THE NORTH ATLANTIC, SHOWING COMPARATIVE DISTANCES

42/-
6903
£2.10

ATLANTIC BRIDGEHEAD
THE STORY OF TRANSATLANTIC COMMUNICATIONS

Howard Clayton

ATLANTIC BRIDGEHEAD

THE STORY OF TRANSATLANTIC COMMUNICATIONS

GARNSTONE PRESS

First published by
THE GARNSTONE PRESS LIMITED
59 Brompton Road, London S.W.3
in 1968

© Howard Clayton 1968

SBN: 900391 11 1

Printed by Billing & Sons Limited, Guildford and London

ACKNOWLEDGEMENTS

Among the many persons and institutions from which I have received help in the preparation of this book I should like particularly to thank the following:

In Newfoundland, Mr. Allen Fraser, Provincial Archivist, and his staff, who placed the resources of their department so readily at my disposal; the Gosling Memorial Library, St. John's, and the Newfoundland Tourist Development Office, both of which supplied information.

I am obliged to the National Library of Canada for finding and copying the relevant parts of the Sandford Fleming Report, and to the Smithsonian Institution in Washington for details and pictures of the U.S.S. *Niagara*.

In Britain the National Maritime Museum, Greenwich, and the Science Museum, South Kensington, have supplied information and illustrations, and I must also thank Mr. H. Appleyard, City Librarian, Lichfield, and his staff for tracking down and obtaining sources of reference.

In the world of business I must thank the Canadian National Railways, whose Chief Archivist, Mr. John Andreasson, supplied much helpful information on railway history; the Marconi Company of Chelmsford, whose Historian, Mr. R. W. Bell, supplied much information and most of the photographs for Chapter 7; the Hunslet Engine Co. of Leeds, the English Electric Co. (Vulcan Foundry) of Newton-le-Willows, and the Bowater Co. of London and Cornerbrook, Newfoundland.

Finally, my thanks are due to two fellow-members of the Canadian Railroad Historical Association, Mr. Ted McQuinn of New Brunswick, and Mr. Tom Norrell of Washington, both of whom have added considerably to my knowledge of the Newfoundland Railway.

HOWARD CLAYTON

CONTENTS

Acknowledgements v
List of illustrations viii
Introduction 11

PART I   THE ATLANTIC TELEGRAPH 15

Chapter 1   The Idea is Born 17
2   First Attempt—the 1858 Cable 32
3   The *Great Eastern's* Cable, 1865 56
4   Success 75

PART II   THE GREAT AMERICAN AND EUROPEAN SHORT LINE RAILWAY 81

Chapter 5   Sandford Fleming and His Vision 83
6   The Reality—The Newfoundland Railway 104

PART III   MARCONI AND HIS WIRELESS 131

Chapter 7   The First Transatlantic Wireless Message 133

PART IV   CONQUEST OF THE ATLANTIC BY AIR 151

Chapter 8   The *Daily Mail* Prize—First Attempts 153
9   Alcock and Brown Win the Prize 169
10   The Atlantic is Conquered 183

Index 190

LIST OF ILLUSTRATIONS

Map of the North Atlantic   *Endpapers*

Between pages

1 Queen's Battery, Signal Hill, St John's, with harbour and city in the background and the narrows on the left   32–33
2 Newfoundland Telegraph Station, 1855
3 Cape Race, terminus of the American telegraph system, 1864
4 H.M.S. *Agamemnon* and U.S.S. *Niagara* reloading cable at Devonport
5 Bay Bulls Arm Cable Station, as drawn in 1858
6 Thompson's Mirror Speaking Galvonometer (1858)
7 Facsimile of the first public message sent through the Atlantic cable
8 The screw engine room of *Great Eastern*
9 Examining the cable for a flaw
10 A deck view of *Great Eastern*
11 The paddle engine room of *Great Eastern*
12 Cable machinery on *Great Eastern*
13 *Great Eastern* at sea   64–65
14 Landing the shore end of the cable, Foilhummeran Bay, Ireland, 1865
15 Sandford Fleming's scheme for an intercontinental route (map)
16 Locomotive *A. L. Blackman*, Newfoundland Railway, 1882
17 Locomotive *St. John's*, Newfoundland Railway, 1882
18 Locomotive *193*, Reid Newfoundland Railway, 1920
19 Harbour Grace from the Railway, about 1900
20 Derailment of locomotive near King's Bridge Road, St. John's
21 Locomotive *193* preserved at Bowater Park, Cornerbrook, 1967
22 St. John's Railway Station

		Between pages
23	Locomotive 939 (diesel electric), Newfoundland Railway	64–65
24	Bowater Pulp and Paper Mills, Cornerbrook	128–129
25	Cabot Tower, Signal Hill, St. John's, Newfoundland	
26	Wireless apparatus used in early experiments by Sir Oliver Lodge	
27	Thornycroft Steam Bus used by Marconi as a mobile wireless receiver	
28	The Poldhu transmitter	
29	Circular Aerial Array, Poldhu	
30	Fan-shaped Aerial Array, Poldhu, in 1901	
31	Marconi with his assistants, Kemp and Paget, at Cabot Tower	
32	Marconi, Kemp and Paget inside Cabot Tower	160–161
33	Preparing to fly one of the aerial kites on Signal Hill	
34	Sir Cavendish Boyle (Governor), Sir Robert Bond (Prime Minister), and members of the Cabinet, with Marconi December 17th, 1901	
35	Marconi with some of his receiving apparatus at Signal Hill	
36	Marconi Memorial, Signal Hill, St. John's	
37	The Vickers *Vimy* at Lester's Field before the transatlantic flight	
38	Alcock and Brown taking off from Lester's Field, June 14th, 1919	
39	The statue of Sir John Alcock and Sir Arthur Whitten Brown at London Airport	

I am grateful to the following for their permission to reproduce illustrations in this book: The Bowater Organisation (24), Central Office of Information (39), Hunslet Engine Co. Ltd. (16), *Illustrated London News* (3, 4), The Marconi Company Ltd. (27, 28, 29, 30, 31, 32, 33, 34, 35), the Trustees of the National Maritime Museum (8, 9, 10, 11, 12, 14), the Newfoundland Tourist Development Office (1, 25, 36), the Science Museum, London (6, 26, 37, 38), and Sir Leonard Outerbridge, C.B.E., D.S.O. (19).

ix

INTRODUCTION

THE ISLAND OF Newfoundland is situated between the latitudes of 46° 36′ and 51° 39′ north, and between longitudes of 52° 37′ and 59° 24′ west. It lies at the mouth of the Gulf of St. Lawrence, and because of its geographical similarity to that country, has often been called 'the Norway of the New World'. Certainly the Norsemen who crossed the Atlantic and came to its shores a thousand years ago must have found themselves in strangely familiar surroundings. Its coast is a mass of inlets and fiords; one third of its surface is water, and from the air the prevailing impression is of rocks and pine forests stretching as far as the eye can see.

Over much of the island's surface there is no sign of man's works, and this is hardly surprising, for although Newfoundland is almost the size of England, its population is only half a million. Most of these are of English or Irish descent, the English settlers coming from the West Country. Until recently their main occupations were fishing and lumbering, and their lives were hard and living often precarious. Yet in spite of this Newfoundlanders have a pride in their country and an attachment to it not surpassed anywhere in the world.

Newfoundland is triangular in shape. Down its west side runs a ridge of mountains, rising at times to 2,000 feet. The eastern end of the island is flat, and at its extremity is the Avalon Peninsula, where nearly half the population lives. Here, facing out across the broad wastes of the Atlantic towards the continent of Europe, is the capital, St. John's. It lies around the edge of a land-locked harbour, approached through the 'Narrows', a passage 700 feet wide in the 400 feet high cliffs—one of the most dramatic harbour entrances in the world. Through the Narrows generations of Newfoundland seamen have set sail, in spring for the sealing grounds and in summer to catch the cod which later they will carry, dried and salted, to countries as far away as Portugal on the one hand, and Brazil on the other. Together with fogs, codfish is the subject which comes first to people's minds if you mention Newfoundland to them. But codfish has not the importance it once had, and of that which is caught today, more is frozen than dried.

Newfoundland's real significance in the world lies in its unique position. It is, except for Greenland, the most easterly part of the North American continent, being about 1,800 miles from Ireland. It lies on the great circle followed by ships crossing the North Atlantic and for those coming from the east is their first landfall; many times in its history the harbour of St. John's has provided a haven for ships struggling disabled through Atlantic gales.

It is not surprising, therefore, that the first Europeans to land in America came to Newfoundland. About the year 1018 Leif Ericson and his Vikings landed in the north of the island, and nearly 500 years later, in 1497, the island was rediscovered by John Cabot, who had set out from Bristol seeking new lands in the west for Henry VII. In 1578 it became Britain's first colony when Sir Humphrey Gilbert took possession of it in the name of Queen Elizabeth I, and throughout the seventeenth and eighteenth centuries it was defended, first against the Dutch and later against the French. Today, on either side of the Narrows, can still be seen the great iron ringbolts from which, in time of war, a chain was hung to keep enemy ships from entering the harbour, while on the heights above, where in 1901 Marconi received the first wireless message to cross the Atlantic, ancient cannon still cover the approaches to St. John's. Around these guns, on September 13th, 1762, British troops under Colonel Amherst fought and defeated, for the last time on Newfoundland soil, the French invaders. Thus ended the last attempt by France to dominate the island, with its strategic position at the mouth of the St. Lawrence, a position which once again came into prominence during the second world war when St. John's became a nerve centre for Atlantic convoys and anti-submarine warfare. That, however, is another story.

This book is concerned with a different side of Newfoundland's history. Not only has its position been of strategic importance in war, but even more has it been so in peace. With its unique position, it has been the obvious western link in any attempt to develop communications between the Old World and the New. When a transatlantic cable became feasible, it was natural that its western end should terminate in Newfoundland; so too, it was the obvious point at which to receive the first transatlantic wireless transmissions. When man first thought of attempting to fly the Atlantic it was natural that Newfoundland should be the springboard for his attempts. So the country has played a vital part in the history of

INTRODUCTION

world communications, and in striking contrast to its own internal isolation, has been thrust into contact with the greater world outside.

The story of these attempts, which I have tried to set out in this book, is a fascinating one for two reasons. Firstly, because it shows pioneers in a completely new field, feeling their way in a technical darkness. Secondly, it is a record of human endeavour such as we are unlikely ever to see again. The driving force behind all these projects consisted of a few men: Cyrus Field; Marconi; Alcock and Brown. They not only had the vision to see the possibility of what they attempted, but the will and persistence to carry it through. Today, in the field of communications, we are literally moving into new worlds and there seems to be no end to the wonders that science can achieve. But this is now the province of nations, and a few wealthy ones at that. Planning is done by committees, finance is raised by governments, and the execution is carried out by military services. The field has become too vast for individual action.

And so, too, we have lost the capacity to wonder, as one miracle of science succeeds another. It is hard now to imagine how our forefathers must have felt. For thousands of years messages had travelled only as fast as a man could travel, and even steam-power had only speeded up the process. Then, suddenly, instantaneous communication became possible with men on the other side of the world. In 1858, when the first Atlantic cable was landed, Newfoundland was two or three weeks by sea from England, and suddenly, one day, it was in direct communication with Europe. It was, indeed, something to wonder at.

In the Newfoundland Museum at St. John's, there is a section devoted to the history of the Atlantic telegraph. There, amid sections of cable, galvanometers, and other instruments, is a small harmonium. On it, an inscribed brass plate states that at Heart's Content, on July 27th, 1866, the harmonium was taken down to the beach and used to accompany a Te Deum on the occasion of the successful completion of the laying of the transatlantic cable. To the people of that time it was, indeed, a miracle.

PART ONE
THE ATLANTIC TELEGRAPH

CHAPTER 1

The Idea is Born

THE UNIQUE POSITION of Newfoundland as the nearest point in North America to the continent of Europe, and its consequent potentialities as a link in transatlantic communications system must have been apparent to many from the earliest days of the 19th century. Even when steam invaded the North Atlantic, New York was still twelve days or more from Liverpool, while St. John's was only seven or eight. But this was of little use to the traveller on his way to the mainland, for from St. John's inland for more than 300 miles the interior was an unexplored wilderness of forest, swamp, and lake with not a road or track to follow. In 1822 W. E. Cormack crossed the country from east to west, one of the few white men to do so, and described his adventures in his *Narrative of a Journey across the Island of Newfoundland*. It took him and his companions six weeks, and the only inhabitants of the country they met were caribou and brown bears. This is how Cormack described his first view of the interior:

'On looking towards the sea coast, the scene was magnificent. We discovered that, under the cover of the forest, we had been uniformly ascending ever since we left the salt water at Random Bar, and then soon arrived at the summit of what we saw to be a great mountain ridge, that seems to act as a barrier between the sea and the interior. The black dense forest through which we had pilgrimaged presented a novel picture, appearing spotted with bright yellow marshes, and a few glassy lakes in its bosom, some of which we had passed close by without seeing them.

'In the westwards, to our inexpressible delight, the interior broke in sublimity before us. What a contrast did this present to the conjectures entertained of Newfoundland! The hitherto mysterious interior lay before us, a boundless scene—emerald surface—a vast basin. The eye strides again and again over a succession of northerly and southerly ranges of green plains marbled with woods and lakes of every form and extent.'

Later in his narrative Cormack describes the centre of the island as follows:

'September 11th—We descended into the bosom of the interior. The plains which shone so brilliantly are steppes or savannas composed of fine black compact peat mould, formed by the growth and decay of mosses. They are in the form of extensive, gently undulating beds, stretching northwards and southwards, with running water and lakes skirted with woods lying between them. Their yellow-green surfaces are sometimes uninterrupted by either tree, shrub, rock, or any irregularity, for more than ten miles. They are chequered everywhere upon the surface by deep beaten deer paths, and are in reality magnificent natural deer parks, adorned with wood and water.

'Our progress over the savanna country was attended with great labour and consequently slow, being at the rate of from five to seven miles a day to the westward, while the distance we walked was three or four times as much.'

Under these conditions, the traveller who landed at St. John's en route for the mainland had no alternative but to continue his journey by sea. The same applied to messages, as long as these had to be carried by hand. Until it could be crossed, the interior of Newfoundland was a greater barrier than the Atlantic itself.

In 1837, however, there occurred an event which was to open up amazing opportunities for communication throughout the world. In June of that year in England, Charles Wheatstone and William Cooke were granted a patent for an electric telegraph. During the autumn they laid an experimental line between Euston and Camden Town on the London and Birmingham Railway. This telegraph had five wires, which were laid in grooves cut in lengths of timber, the grooves being filled with pitch and the timbers buried beside the railway line.* At either end of this telegraph was one of Wheatstone's five-needle telegraph instruments. The experiment was successful,

---

* A piece of this timber, with the wires still embedded in it, was dug up at Euston sixty years later and can be seen today in the Science Museum, South Kensington.

and in the following year a permanent telegraph line was installed on the Great Western Railway between London and Slough, a distance of twenty-one miles. This consisted of an 'air-line', that is, wires suspended from insulators on poles; the instruments used were Wheatstone's two-needle indicators which required only two wires, and thus was set the pattern for the electric telegraph for many years to come. Telegraph lines grew rapidly all over the world, causing a revolution in the passing of news.

It was obvious to many in Newfoundland that here was the opportunity to make use of the country's unique position. A telegraph line could cross the wilderness of the Newfoundland interior, could link up with other lines across Canada and the United States, and messages from all over the American continent would arrive at St. John's for onward transmission by steamer to Europe in six or seven days. The idea did not yet extend to a submarine cable across the Atlantic; that was to come later.

No doubt many people thought like this, but the credit for being the first to put his thoughts into print must go to Dr. J. T. Mullock, a Roman Catholic Bishop of Newfoundland. This worthy prelate, like many other reverend gentlemen before and after him, had a great interest in the application of electricity and steam-power to problems of communication. Nor was his interest merely academic; for many years he preached the doctrine that the prosperity of Newfoundland and its people could be improved immeasurably by modern communications, and he championed in turn the cause of the electric telegraph, steamships, and the railway. On at least one occasion his zeal in this direction carried him too far. For many years he had advocated a regular steamship service around the coasts of Newfoundland, communicating with the outports, or fishing villages. In 1860, while on a visit to New York he saw a steamer, the *Victoria*, which he judged to be ideal for this purpose. Without any more ado, and without any consultation, he virtually made a charter with the owners of the steamer on behalf of the Newfoundland Government, to run the vessel around the coasts twice a month. Not unnaturally, when the Government heard of this matter, they repudiated the action of their unauthorised agent, and for some time Dr. Mullock and the administration were, to use trade union jargon, 'in dispute'. It is significant, however, that the following year the *Victoria* was (officially) on government charter.

Long before this, however, Dr. Mullock had brought to the fore the question of telegraph communication. In 1850 he had written the following letter to the Editor of the New York *Courier*.

'To the Editor of The Courier   St. John's, Nov. 8, 1850.
'I regret to find that in every plan for Transatlantic Communication, Halifax is always mentioned, and the natural capabilities of Newfoundland entirely overlooked. This has been deeply impressed on my mind by the communication I read in your newspaper of Saturday last, regarding telegraphic communication between England and Ireland, in which it was said that the nearest telegraphic station on the American side is Halifax, twenty-one hundred and fifty-five miles from the coast of Ireland. Now would it not be well to call the attention of England and America to the extraordinary capabilities of St. John's as the nearest telegraphic point? It is an Atlantic port, lying I may say, in the track of the ocean steamers, and by establishing it as the American telegraphic station, news could be communicated to the whole American continent forty-eight hours, at least, sooner than by any other route. But how will this be accomplished? Just look at the map of Newfoundland and Cape Breton. From St. John's to Cape Ray there is no difficulty in establishing a line passing near Holy-Rood along the neck of land connecting Trinity and Placentia Bays and thence in a direction due west to the Cape. You have then about forty-one to forty-five miles of sea to St. Paul's Island with deep soundings, of one hundred fathoms, so that the electric cable will be perfectly safe from icebergs. Thence, to Cape North, in Cape Breton, is little more than twelve miles. Thus it is not only practicable to bring America two days nearer to Europe by this route, but should the telegraphic communication between England and Ireland, 62 miles, be realised, it presents not the least difficulty. Of course, we in Newfoundland will have nothing to do with the erection, working and maintenance of the telegraph; but I suppose our Government will give every facility to the company, either English or American, who will undertake it, as it will be an incalculable advantage to this country. I hope the day is not far distant when St. John's will be the first link in the electric chain which will unite the Old World and the New.'

Bishop Mullock had not long to wait. The following year, 1851,

Newfoundland had a visit from one of the pioneers of electric telegraphy, Frederic Newton Gisborne. A native of Manchester, he had worked on several of the earliest telegraph lines in Canada, and was at this time engineer of the Nova Scotia Telegraph Company. His purpose in coming to Newfoundland was to build the St John's and Carbonear Electric Telegraph Company's line. This was a purely internal line to a point in Conception Bay, about eighty miles from St. John's. Later on, when the Atlantic cable was landed nearby, the Carbonear line became an important link in the transatlantic route.

While working on this line, Mr. Gisborne appeared before the Newfoundland Legislature to explain a plan which he had prepared. It was, in fact, that outlined by Bishop Mullock in his letter; a telegraph line from St. John's to Cape Ray to connect with Cape Breton by carrier pigeon or steamer and eventually by submarine cable. The Legislature were impressed by the suggestions of this expert; they voted £500 for a survey and passed an act authorising Mr. Gisborne to form a company for the purpose of building a line.

He lost no time in carrying out his project. Between September 4th and December 4th he completed his survey through 350 miles of woods and wilderness. One of his party of six died and the rest were at times near starvation, but by the end he had established a practicable route. In accordance with the provisions of the Act, it had to consist of a path not less than four feet in width and open to the public with suitable bridges over waterways, running alongside the telegraph line for maintenance purposes.

In the spring of 1852 a further Act was passed incorporating the 'Newfoundland Electric Telegraph Company' with exclusive right to erect telegraphs in the island for the next thirty years, and a grant of land at the completion of the line to Cape Ray. The authorised capital was £100,000, in shares of £100, and Gisborne departed for New York to raise the money.

He appears to have had some difficulty in doing so, for the new company did not get started on its project for another year, and those who did promise to subscribe the capital were to turn out to be broken reeds. During this year, however, Gisborne went to England and purchased a length of submarine cable which he laid in November 1852 from Prince Edward Island to New Brunswick. This was the first submarine cable to be laid in America, and it brought

Newfoundland a step nearer to telegraphic contact with the mainland.

Throughout the summer in 1853 work progressed on the construction of the land line. So rugged did Gisborne find the terrain that he decided to place the line underground. In doing so he may also have been guided by his experience on the St. John's–Carbonear line, where complaints of malicious damage were frequent. The outport boys of those days could not resist the temptation to throw stones, or in the vernacular 'to fire rocks', at the glass insulators.

Some forty miles had been laid when the blow fell. The company's funds failed; Gisborne's bills were dishonoured by his New York agents and he himself lost all he possessed. Work on the telegraph line came to an abrupt halt, and so ended the brief history of the Newfoundland Electric Telegraph Company.

Undaunted, Gisborne returned to New York to raise new funds. There, in January 1854 he met Matthew Field, a merchant, who introduced him to his brother Cyrus. Cyrus Field, then only 33, had already retired after a successful business career as a paper manufacturer. The youngest of seven sons, in a family of Puritan descent, he had begun his career in a New York mercantile office for one dollar a week at the age of fifteen. In eighteen years he had made a fortune, and was now looking for other fields in which his tremendous vitality, pertinacity, and organising ability could be put to use. Gisborne's project caught his imagination; and from the first he saw the wider possibilities of the scheme. He invited Gisborne to his house and when, after an evening's conversation, Gisborne had left, Cyrus Field walked over to the globe standing in a corner of his library in order to visualise the scheme. It was then that he recalled a conversation he had had some ten years previously with Professor Morse. Samuel Morse has been immortalised by the signal code which bears his name, but he is equally entitled to fame as the builder of America's first telegraph. While Wheatstone and Cooke were at work in England, Morse was working on similar lines in America, and his first telegraph was completed with government aid in 1843. He was a pioneer of telegraphy in America, and inventor of the telegraph magnetic recorder.

Morse's remark, which Field now remembered, was that 'a telegraphic communication might with certainty be established across the Atlantic Ocean'. Field's imagination was fired, and at once he took hold of the larger idea of cable communication with Europe, while Gisborne's limited idea of a line across Newfoundland was forgotten. Here was just such a project as he had been looking for, on which he could exercise his organising talents and his financial power.

He wasted no time, but the following days sent off two letters: one to Professor Morse enquiring as to the possibility of sending electrical impulses over such a vast distance, and the other to Lieut. Matthew F. Maury, head of the National Observatory at Washington and one of the foremost authorities on oceanography, whom he questioned on the submarine conditions likely to be encountered.

The replies to both letters were encouraging. Lieut. Maury had information from a survey carried out the year before between Newfoundland and Ireland in anticipation of just such a project as the Atlantic cable. It showed that the 1,600 miles stretch of ocean consisted of a plateau with a maximum depth of 2,070 fathoms; deep enough for the cable to clear ships' anchors and icebergs, but shallow enough to make the project feasible. Lieut. Maury was cautious as to the practicability of the project, though, ending his report with the words 'I do not, however, pretend to consider the question as the possibility of a time calm enough, a sea smooth enough, a wire long enough, or a ship big enough, to lay a coil of wire sixteen hundred miles in length'.

Professor Morse showed even greater interest and suggested a meeting in New York to discuss the question. This was arranged, and so began a friendship between Morse and Field that was to last for a lifetime. Morse not only stated his opinion that the transatlantic cable was feasible, but offered his great knowledge and experience of electrical telegraphy to help in the project. Field's mind was made up: he decided to go ahead; and thus began one of the greatest enterprises in modern history.

His first act was to gather around him a group of fellow-businessmen who were prepared to risk their money in this gigantic speculation. It must be realised that, as in the case of the early railways, there was no lack of self-considered experts who were ready to prove, without the slightest hesitation, that the whole scheme was impossible. It was true that some years before (1851), John and Jacob Brett had successfully laid and operated a submarine cable across the English Channel, but the doubters were quick to point out the difference between thirty miles and 1,600. It is a tribute to the force of Cyrus Field's personality and to his indefatigable enthusiasm that he was able to find five financiers who were willing not only to find the initial half a million pounds to start the scheme, but who would support him thoughout the twelve years of heartbreaking set-backs and disappointments that they were to experience before the project was completed. During this time they had to find a further £1,000,000 over and above the original amount, and until the twelve years had elapsed the return on this huge outlay was negligible. The names of Field's associates who with him made up the 'five immortals', as they came to be known, were Peter Cooper, Moses Taylor, Marshall Roberts and Chandler White. Later, they were joined by a sixth, Wilson Hunt.

After the first meeting of the group it was decided to send Field and Chandler White to Newfoundland to seek a charter. The Newfoundland Electric Telegraph Company agreed to surrender its charter, and the Newfoundland Government were then approached with regard to a new one. So persuasive was Field that the Legislative Assembly not only agreed unanimously, but offered £50,000 in bonds towards the project. An Act was passed incorporating a new company, to be named the 'New York, Newfoundland, and London Telegraph Company'. It took over the rights of the old company and in addition was granted the sole right to land cables and receive telegraphic messages in Newfoundland for fifty years. Neither the Newfoundland Government nor the company could have been expected to foresee the complications that might ensue from this clause, but it later became the subject of litigation, for the fifty years was sufficient to reach into the era of wireless telegraphy and the cable company suddenly experienced competition from an unexpected source.

The New York, Newfoundland and London Company, once formed, paid off the debts of the old company and took over such assets as still remained, including the forty miles of route which had been completed. With this final winding up of the company that he had started, Frederic Gisborne vanishes from the picture and is heard of no more. The part he played as the man who started it all has been largely forgotten, and his name overshadowed by the giants who completed what he had begun. It is pleasing to know, however, that the people of Newfoundland did not forget him. Gisborne's exertions had ensured that for many years to come the transatlantic telegraph would pass through Newfoundland to the material benefit of the island. The citizens of St. John's expressed their appreciation in the manner which was considered appropriate at the time, as the following extract from the *Manchester Examiner and Times* shows.

'Testimonial to Mr. F. N. Gisborne
'A very beautiful, valuable, and appropriate piece of plate has been prepared as a testimonial to Mr. Frederic Newton Gisborne, eldest son of Hartley P. Gisborne Esq., of this city, contributed and to be presented by the inhabitants of St. John's, Newfoundland, as marking their sense of the energy and perseverance he has displayed in traversing the previously unexplored parts of the island in anticipation of the introduction of the electric telegraph. The design is bold, and highly characteristic of the subject portrayed. At the summit of a rocky eminence, in frosted silver, stands a figure of science, with a wreath of immortelles in her upraised and extended left hand, ready to crown the deserving enterprise—a figure of Roman character, with a hatchet in one hand, evincing vigour and determination, and in the other a pair of compasses, indicative of skill and calculation has struggled nearly to the highest point, and is handing the compasses to science. The rocky heights are studded here and there with North-American fir trees. Upon the front of the base an oval is formed by a cable and within the coil is the inscription; on the opposite side is represented a vessel at sea laying down the cable for the electric telegraph. A group of seals and a group of beavers occupy part of the space between these. There is also engraved representations of American scenery, with Indian wig-wams. The specific character of the testimonial is further indicated by the whole being encircled by telegraph posts and wires. Manchester may justly take some credit to itself on account of its relation to the gentleman whose enterprise this testimonial commemorates.'

One hopes that Mr. Gisborne appreciated this piece of typical Victorian exuberance. He certainly had earned it.

While his associates were busy settling the affairs of the company in St. John's and getting work started again on the land-line, Cyrus

Field departed for England, to see about the manufacture of the submarine cable which would be used between Newfoundland and Cape Breton. On arrival he consulted John Brett, the man responsible for the laying of the first cable across the English Channel in 1851, and was recommended by him to the two firms who had manufactured it. These were the Gutta Percha Company of London who made the core of the cable, and Glass, Elliott and Company of Greenwich, wire rope manufacturers, who made the outside. From the first of these two firms Field commissioned the short length of cable required to link Newfoundland with the mainland, and thus set the pattern for future Anglo-American co-operation on the transatlantic cables. While Field and his associates in America organised the project and supplied most of the capital, Britain contributed the cable itself, the instruments required to work it and the technical knowledge. The British, at this time, had already established a lead in submarine telegraphy which has been maintained to this day. As an example of this, the Newfoundland–Cape Breton cable was the first one in the world to be made with a stranded core, an important advance which added considerably to its strength and consequent ease of laying.

While in Britain Field took the opportunity of discussing his project with several British engineers who already had some experience of submarine telegraphy. As well as John Brett he met Charles Bright, who, at the age of 20, had become Chief Engineer of the Magnetic Telegraph Company. He was one of the foremost telegraph engineers of his time, and was later to be knighted for the part he played in the Atlantic cable. Both of these men were later to join Field's enterprise.

By October 1856 the cable was ready for laying between Newfoundland and Cape Breton, and Field and his associates arrived to watch the proceedings. The cable had been brought from England in the sailing barque *Sarah L. Bryant*, and it was now to be laid from that vessel under tow by the company's paddle-steamer *Victoria*. It was not a satisfactory arrangement and it is not surprising that the attempt came to grief. During the laying a storm sprang up, and the captain of the *Sarah L. Bryant*, tethered at stem and stern, had to cut the telegraph cable to save his ship. This was the first of many such disappointments and setbacks.

Field now had to turn his attention to the land-line from St.

John's to Cape Ray. This had been completed the previous year, with its 4-foot pathway. It did not strike across the island in a straight line, but ran parallel to the south coast, a few miles inland to avoid the many inlets. In this way it had been possible to keep the working parties supplied by sea. The cost of building the line had been heavy, $1,000,000 having been expended, much of which had been due to waste and mismanagement. In his *History of Newfoundland* Judge Prowse recalls how, as a young man, he watched the crew of the *Victoria* unloading glass insulators at Burgeo for the telegraph. By the time they were landed three out of every five of the insulators were smashed; 'There goes another ten cents of Peter Cooper's,' a seaman would shout. Although the telegraph line had been completed only a year it was already out of order. Maintenance work was disorganised and operators had not been trained. The manager, Simpson, had resigned in despair at a job which was too big for him.

One of the marks of the successful administrator is the ability to select his subordinates so that he has the right man for every job, and Cyrus Field was no exception to this rule. He made enquiries from independent sources to find the best telegraph engineer in North America. They were unanimous in recommending A. M. Mackay, Chief Electrician of the Nova Scotia Telegraph Co. Although only 22 years of age he had already achieved a considerable reputation in his profession.

Mackay accepted the post of manager of the New York, Newfoundland and London Telegraph Company in Newfoundland. He set to work at once, and with the primitive means then available raised the end of the Cape Breton cable and completed laying it, thus connecting Newfoundland with the mainland by telegraph. He then set out to walk the length of the land-line to St. John's, supervising the maintenance work as he went. Having put the line in order he set about training operators, and before long had an efficient telegraph system working from St. John's to the Canadian mainland, and thence to the whole of the American continent. The task which Gisborne had set out to do had at last been accomplished. It had taken five years to do it.

Mackay stayed on in Newfoundland as manager and rendered valuable service to the company. Throughout the ensuing seven years, while the world waited for the completion of the transatlantic link, he kept the Newfoundland telegraph in an efficient state for the day when it would be required, and later rebuilt the entire line at far less than its original cost. Later in life he entered politics, and was elected to the House of Assembly of Newfoundland.

With the completion of the line to St. John's it was possible to use it to a limited extent for communication with Europe. Transatlantic steamers passed close to Cape Race, some miles south of St. John's, and the Associated Press kept a boat at Cape Race which regularly met incoming and outgoing ships. Incoming despatches, with the latest news of the European continent, were thrown overboard in a water-tight canister with a flag attached, to be picked up by the news-boat. Outgoing despatches were transferred in the same containers, from the news-boat to the ship by means of a pick up net, in the same manner as the travelling post office on the railway. The first ship to take part in this 'tin-can mail' was the S.S. *Vigo* of the Inman line, and from 1859 until the completion of the cable seven years later, day in and day out, in fair weather and foul, the news-boat in charge of bold John Murphy kept up this service. To readers of the daily papers in New York and London the heading 'By telegraph via Cape Race' became a familiar sight, but few, no doubt, even stopped to think what this meant.

While work had been going on to establish the telegraph link as far as St. John's, Field had been directing his attention to the question of the Atlantic cable. Early in 1856, he had been to Washington to ask the United States Government to make a further survey of the route, and this was done by Lieut. Berryman in July of that year. In three weeks he surveyed the route from west to east between Newfoundland and Ireland. Soundings were taken every twenty miles, using an apparatus specially devised by Lieut. Berryman for the purpose. This consisted of an open tube suspended vertically at the end of the sounding line. The tube was passed through a hole drilled through a large cannon ball in such a way that the cannon ball could slide easily up and down the tube. It was held in a central position by two wires attached to hooks at the top of the tube, and acted as a weight carrying the tube vertically downwards until it hit the sea bottom. When this happened and the weight came off the line, the hooks released the cannon ball and the tube could be drawn up by itself, with a sample of the sea bottom inside it. Lieut. Berryman's course across the Atlantic is, presumably, to this day marked by a line of cannon balls resting on the sea bottom at twenty-mile intervals!

Not content with one survey Field requested the British Government to make a further one from east to west, and this was done by Lieut. Commander Dayman in H.M.S. *Cyclops*. This confirmed Lieut. Berryman's findings; that the route traversed an undersea plateau (later to be named the Telegraphic Plateau) with a maximum depth of 14,000 feet, or just over two and a half miles, and having a soft floor of diatomaceae and globigerinae ooze, 'a veritable feather bed' in the words of Lieut. Berryman. Conditions for a submarine cable could hardly have been better.

Much of this time Field spent in England. It is interesting to note that in this period, up to the final laying of the cable, he made forty Atlantic crossings and this at a time when a crossing took anything up to twelve days—well over a year spent at sea in fact! In England he consulted every authority he could find. As well as those already mentioned—John Brett and Charles Bright—he conferred with Samuel Canning, Chief Engineer of Glass, Elliot and Co.; Robert Stephenson the famous railway engineer; and the equally famous Isambard Brunel. The latter took Field down to the Isle of Dogs, on the Thames, where Brunel's mammoth ship the *Great Eastern* was building. 'There,' said the great engineer, pointing to the huge bulk of his ship rising on the stocks, 'there, Mr. Field, is the ship to lay your Atlantic cable.'

These were prophetic words, for the *Great Eastern*, so much in advance of her time that she failed in almost all else, did in fact eventually prove the answer to the problem of laying Field's cable. Before that came about, however, much was to happen.

In the autumn of 1856 Field was joined in England by Professor Morse. Through the good offices of Charles Bright, Morse was able to carry out an important experiment with the help of the Magnetic Telegraph Co. This company owned most of the rapidly extending telegraph system of the United Kingdom and many of their principal lines were laid underground, using cables similar to a submarine telegraph. One night, after commercial working had ceased, Morse was present in the office of the Magnetic Telegraph Co. at Broad Street in London when ten cables with a total length of 1,000 miles were joined together in series. Throughout the night signals were sent and received over this continuous length with complete success.

Field was now satisfied that it was technically possible to lay the cable and to work it when that was accomplished. The next move was to approach the two governments concerned. He first wrote to Lord Clarendon, British Foreign Secretary, outlining his proposals and seeking an interview. The resulting conference was encouraging. The British Government, with its growing overseas commitments, fully realised the value of the telegraph in general and the Atlantic cable in particular. Lord Clarendon was able to offer the use of vessels of the Royal Navy and a government subsidy of £14,000 per year once the cable was in use. When the profits reached a figure equal to 6 per cent on the capital the subsidy would fall to £10,000 for a further twenty-five years. In return the British Government were to have priority in the use of the telegraph over all users except the United States Government. Field accepted this offer on behalf of his company and the necessary government bill was put in hand and became law on July 20th, 1857.

It was not so easy to convince the United States Government of the value of the project. After considerable dissent in Congress, the enabling Act was only passed by a narrow majority. It provided for a subsidy of $70,000 per annum, falling to $50,000 when the profits reached 6 per cent, as in the British case. This Act was passed on March 3rd, 1857.

Up till now the project had been financed by Field and his colleagues, who had expended £1,500,000 in taking the telegraph as far as St. John's. Field now decided that the time had come to raise additional capital in Britain, and for this purpose to form another company in that country. Accordingly, on September 29th, 1856, Cyrus Field, John Brett, and Charles Bright met and drew up the following agreement:

'Mutually, and on equal terms, we engage to exert ourselves for the purpose of forming a company for establishing and working of electric telegraph communications between Newfoundland and Ireland, such company to be called the "Atlantic Telegraph Company", or any such name as the parties shall jointly agree upon.'

The new company was duly formed after a meeting at Liverpool, and in a few weeks the authorised capital of £350,000 was subscribed. The shares consisted of 350 of £1,000 each, and over a quarter of them were taken by Field. Of the remainder, the majority was purchased by shareholders of the Magnetic Telegraph Co. among whom there was considerable support for the project.

The object of the Atlantic Telegraph Company was to continue the work of the New York, Newfoundland, and London Telegraph Company by laying and operating a submarine cable between Newfoundland and Ireland. In due course, when the project had been completed, the two companies became amalgamated, under the title of 'The Anglo-American Telegraph Company'. This, however, was still some years ahead.

So now the stage had been set for the final and most important act. In the American continent the telegraph had stretched out its tentacle until it had reached the eastern extremity at St. John's. On the European side, the Magnetic Telegraph Company had worked its way westward to Valentia, on the west coast of Ireland. The possibility of spanning the gap by a submarine cable had been established; the approval of governments on both sides of the ocean secured; and a company formed to carry out the project. After five years all was ready.

CHAPTER 2

First Attempt—the 1858 Cable

THE FORMATION OF the Atlantic Telegraph Company at the close of 1856 brought together an impressive array of talent. The directors, in addition to Field, Brett and Bright, included William Thompson, Professor of Natural Philosophy at Glasgow University, who was later to become world famous as Lord Kelvin, and who contributed greatly to the eventual success of the enterprise. Officers of the company included Mr. Charles Bright as Chief Engineer, and Dr. William Wildman Whitehouse as Electrician (the term as used at this time denoted an electrical consultant rather than a technician). Dr. Whitehouse was a physician who had studied electricity as a hobby. Although a brilliant theorist, his practical application of his knowledge was not of such a high standard, and the company had eventually to dispense with his services after several disastrous efforts on his part.

In their anxiety to lay the cable during the summer of 1857, the directors placed the order for it almost immediately. Three firms were involved, the core being made by the Gutta Percha Company, and the outer covering put on it by two firms, Messrs. Glass, Elliot and Co. of Greenwich, and Messrs. Newall & Co. of Birkenhead. Unfortunately, in their haste the directors allowed far too little time for experiment and for testing the cable. As one result of this it was found, when the cable came to be laid, that the two firms manufacturing the outer covering had each made it with the armouring, or outer covering of iron wire, laid in a different direction, a factor which caused considerable difficulty when the two parts had to be spliced together.

The cable consisted of a core of stranded copper weighing 107 lb. per nautical mile covered with gutta percha insulation to a depth of $\frac{3}{8}$ inch. Gutta percha is a substance formed of the latex of certain trees of the Sapotaceae family which grow in the Malay Peninsula. It differs from rubber in being hard and inelastic at ordinary tem-

1 Queen's Battery, Signal Hill, St John's, with harbour and city in the background and the narrows on the left

2   Newfoundland Telegraph Station, 1855

3 Cape Race, terminus of the American telegraph system, 1864

4 H.M.S. *Agamemnon* and U.S.S. *Niagara* reloading cable at Devonport

5   Bay Bulls Arm Cable Station, as drawn in 1858

6   Thompson's Mirror Speaking Galvanometer (1858)

7 Facsimile of the first public message sent through the Atlantic cable

8　The screw engine room of *Great Eastern*

9　Examining the cable for a flaw

10 A deck view of *Great Eastern*

11 The paddle engine room of *Great Eastern*

12 Cable machinery on *Great Eastern*

peratures and in becoming soft and plastic in hot water. It is eminently suitable as an insulator for under-water conductors, its insulating properties increasing under pressure. Its use for submarine cables has only recently been superseded by polyethylene, a synthetic plastic. The method of applying it to a cable as an insulator was invented by Dr. Werner Siemens (another name famous in the history of electrics) who between 1846 and 1849 carried out experiments with machines for extruding the gutta percha around a central conductor, his successful machine being based on those used for making macaroni!

The core was made in lengths of about one to one and a half miles, each length being coiled and immersed in water while the insulation was tested. This was done by Professor Thompson, who found at first that the resistance of the conductor varied. As a result of this he insisted on a standard of purity of the copper used, thus producing a cable of uniform resistance. When the lengths had been joined together to form the two halves of the cable core, he tested the insulation by means of a 500-cell voltaic battery. They were then sent to the two cable factories where they were covered with a helical layer of hempen yarn and armoured with seventeen strands of No. 22 Birmingham Wire Gauge iron wire, giving an overall diameter of $\frac{5}{8}$ inch. As already mentioned, the iron wire was laid with a right hand lay in one half of the cable, and a left hand lay in the other.

It was perhaps inevitable that mistakes would be made in the manufacture of the cable, simply because of the lack of experience and technical knowledge. The principal drawbacks were a low breaking strain and a high specific gravity. The latter characteristic caused the cable to sink too rapidly when being laid, and thus increased the strain on it as it left the ship, especially in an ocean swell. It was unfortunate that the cable had to be made in such a hurry as these drawbacks might have been eliminated if there had been time to experiment. Its total cost was £224,000 and it was completed by July 1857.

As there was no single ship afloat large enough to carry all the cable, it was decided to lay it from two vessels, both warships. The British Government lent H.M.S. *Agamemnon*, and the United States Government the U.S.S. *Niagara*.

The British ship was a battleship of 2,497 tons which had recently taken part in the bombardment of Sebastopol. She was built at

Woolwich between 1849 and 1852 and is said to have been the first battleship designed as a screw vessel, her length being 195 feet and her breadth 54 feet. She belonged to the period of transition from the wooden walls of Nelson to the steam-powered ironclads of the latter half of the nineteenth century, typified by the *Monitor* and *Merrimac* of the American Civil War. The *Agamemnon* was one of the wooden walls with auxiliary steam power. If one imagines Nelson's *Victory*, as she sits at Portsmouth today, with the addition of a screw propeller, and a short funnel between the main and mizzen masts, then one has a fairly accurate picture of H.M.S. *Agamemnon*. Her steam power was purely auxiliary, and the engines only of 600 indicated h.p. The screw was so fitted that it could be hoisted out of the water from the stern when sailing, thus eliminating its drag, and at the same time her funnel could be lowered so as not to obstruct the sails. This accounts for a puzzling feature of pictures of the *Agamemnon*—sometimes she appears to have a funnel and other times she does not. It would be necessary to use the engines all the time, however, when laying cable, and so extra supplies of coal had to be carried which were stowed between decks in bags, or loose behind temporary bulkheads.

The engines of *Agamemnon* were set well aft, and her forepart contained a large hold 45 feet square and 20 feet deep, which it was calculated would hold half her cargo of cable. The rest of her cable was stowed in two large coils, one on the orlop deck, and one on the main deck. Her guns were of course removed, and the gun-ports sealed up.

Her sister ship, the U.S.S. *Niagara*, was a corvette of 5,200 tons and represented a further stage in the transition from wooden wall to ironclad. Her designer George Steers (later to become famous as the builder of the yacht *America* which first carried the America's Cup to the United States) built her as a steamship with auxiliary sail, although of wood. Consequently, she did not experience the same difficulty as *Agamemnon* in carrying enough coal for the voyage, while her extra displacement allowed her to stow all her quota of cable below decks.

Both ships were fitted with apparatus for paying out the cable over the stern, which had been designed and built rather hurriedly by Messrs. C. de Bergue and Co. Retardation of the cable could be effected by a hand-wheel actuating a frame clutch surrounding the outside of a brake-wheel. In addition both vessels were fitted with a 'crinoline' or metal framework around the stern to prevent any possibility of the cable fouling the screw.

When all was ready *Niagara* sailed to Birkenhead and *Agamemnon* to Greenwich, where they proceded to take on cable. This process took three weeks, and required 120 men in each ship. While it was going on, the cable company's officials joined the *Niagara*, which was to lay the first part of the cable. Mr. Charles Bright was the Chief Engineer, with Mr Samuel Canning as his assistant. Dr. Whitehouse was prevented by illness from sailing, and so his place as Chief Electrician was taken by Mr. C. U. de Sauty. Professor Morse accompanied the expedition, but was confined to his berth for the whole voyage.

While these preparations had been going forward, public interest on both sides of the Atlantic had been growing. There were still those who scoffed at the whole idea (Professor Sir George Airy, the Astronomer Royal was one of them), but on the other hand people began to be aware of the tremendous possibilities of this attempt to join the two continents. Their imagination was roused by the immensity of the enterprise and the remarkable lengths to which human ingenuity could reach. The general feeling of the times is admirably summed up in the following remarks made by a prominent American statesman, Edward Everett, in a speech at Albany:

'I hold in my hand a portion of the identical electric cable, given to me by my friend Mr. Peabody, which is now in process of manufacture to connect America with Europe. Does it seem all but incredible to you that intelligence should travel for 2000 miles along these slender copper wires, far down in all but fathomless Atlantic never before penetrated by aught pertaining to humanity save when some foundering vessel has plunged with her hapless company to the eternal silence and darkness of the abyss? Does it seem, I say, all but a miracle of art, that the thoughs of living men—the thoughts that we think up here on the earth's surface, in the cheerful light of day—about the markets and the exchanges, and the seasons and the elections, and the treaties and the wars, and all fond nothings of daily life, should clothe themselves with elemental sparks and shoot with fiery speed in a moment, in a twinkling of an eye, from hemisphere to hemisphere, far down among the uncouth monsters that wallow in the nether seas along the wreck-paved floor, through the oozy dungeons of the rayless deep?'

By August 5th the cable ships had met at Valentia Island, County Kerry. The *Agamemnon* was accompanied by a paddle-steamer H.M.S. *Leopard,* and by the survey ship H.M.S. *Cyclops.* The *Niagara* was attended by another paddle-steamer, the U.S.S. *Susquehanna.* Also present was the tug *Willing Mind* to bring the end of the cable inshore. The members of this fleet quickly nicknamed themselves 'The Wire Squadron'. It had been arranged that *Niagara* should lay the first half of the cable and that *Agamemnon* should take over in mid-ocean. Charles Bright and the other engineers would have preferred to start in mid-ocean, splice the cable, and then steam apart. This would have enabled the ships to wait for fair weather before making the splice, a fairly hazardous operation. They were overruled by the electricians, however, who stressed the necessity of testing the cable to shore continuously, so that the officials on land would know how laying was proceeding. No doubt they were also influenced by the novelty of maintaining communication from ship to shore all the way across the Atlantic.

A vast crowd of people had assembled at Valentia to witness the historic occasion. The Lord Lieutenant of Ireland, the Earl of Carlisle, was there to bestow official blessing on the expedition; celebrated engineers from all over Europe had come to watch the proceedings and sightseers from all around had congregated on the coast.

The shore end of the cable consisted of two miles of extra heavy construction, to stand up to the additional hazards of rocks, ships' anchors, etc. It was brought to land by one of *Niagara's* boats and formally offered by the commander of that ship, Captain Hudson, to the Lord Lieutenant, who in his enthusiasm waded into the water and helped the sailors drag the cable ashore. Speeches followed, and then, according to the custom of the times, a banquet given by the Knight of Kerry. In the nearby village a ball was held which continued until dawn.

The following morning, amid the general air of festivity, *Niagara* got under way and stood out to sea, paying out the cable as she went. After only five miles, however, the cable snapped after being caught up in the paying-out machinery. She hove to, while the submerged cable was under-run by *Willing Mind* and spliced to again.

At first *Niagara* moved slowly, at a mere two knots, to enable her crew to get accustomed to the paying-out procedure. Gradually as the convoy moved out into the broad Atlantic, speed was increased, the vessels keeping within sound of each other's bells. On board *Niagara* there was an unnatural silence. Men walked softly, and spoke in whispers, so great was the tension. As Bright and his assistants watched, the cable-laying machinery rumbled away, the coils came up from below without a kink, and the mysterious-looking cord disappeared over the stern. The weather continued fine, and speed was gradually increased to five knots. All the time the electricians kept testing the cable back to the shore, while messages were passed back to Ireland.

By August 11th (four days out) 380 miles of cable had been laid and all seemed to be going well, when suddenly the mechanic working the brake applied it too hard, the cable parted, and before anything could be done it had run out over the stern. It must be appreciated that the paying-out of the cable required considerable judgment. As the water deepened, the speed at which the cable ran out had to increase above that of the ship, to let out the required slack. At the same time allowance had to be made for drift caused by wind and current, and also for any heavy swell which would cause the ship's stern to rise and fall, thus increasing the strain on the cable. In his report to the directors, on the accident, Bright states that on the next attempt he would ensure that more frequent relays of staff were used and a high degree of skill would be insisted on.

There being no way of raising the broken end of the cable, and there being insufficient length on board to complete the work, the ships returned to Plymouth and discharged their cable in Keyham basin. Thus ended the first attempt to lay the Atlantic Cable. It had been a set-back, but at the same time had shown that when certain difficulties had been overcome, the laying of the cable was perfectly feasible. The projectors of the scheme were by no means disheartened although they had lost the equivalent of £100,000.

During the winter of 1857–58, preparations went ahead for another attempt. A small steamer went to Valentia, recovered fifty miles of the lost cable, and buoyed the shore end ready for splicing on in the coming year. Further capital was raised and additional cable purchased to make up a total of 3,000 miles, thereby providing sufficient surplus to cover all conceivable contingencies. New paying-out machinery was devised and constructed with a self-releasing brake to obviate the possibility of a recurrence of the accident of the first expedition. This device was based on the apparatus used for treadmills in gaols, and was built by the firm of Easton & Amos. It provided for automatic brake-release upon the strain exceeding that intended; this was done by the increased friction between the wheel and the wooden blocks surrounding it causing the wooden blocks to move around with the wheel and so operate the brake lever. Bright also devised a dynamometer to indicate constantly the strain.

By May 29th, 1858, the ships had taken on their cargo of cable again and sailed for the Bay of Biscay. There, about 120 miles north-west of Corunna where the sea has a depth of about three miles, they practised splicing, laying, buoying and picking up cable, using some sections of cable which had been damaged. All went well, and the new machinery worked excellently, a laying speed of seven knots being eventually reached. By June 3rd the 'Wire Squadron' had returned to Plymouth, all ready for their next attempt on the Atlantic. Having coaled and provisioned, they set out on June 10th 'with fair skies and bright prospects'.

This time the plan was to start in mid-ocean, and having spliced the two ends, for the two ships to steam apart, one east and the other west laying cable simultaneously. A rendezvous was therefore arranged for the squadron in lat. 53° 2′ N. and long. 38° 18′ W., and the various ships set out for that point.

The day after starting there was no wind, but on Saturday, June 12th, a breeze sprang up. The *Agamemnon*, with screw hoisted and fires out, bowled along at a rare pace under royals and studding sails. The barometer fell fast and a gale sprang up which was to continue for a week and was very nearly to put an end to the expedition. The worst sufferer from this storm was *Agamemnon*; she was 2,000 tons lighter than *Niagara*, but carried the same weight of cable, a serious handicap in heavy weather. On board her was Nicolas Wood, correspondent of *The Times*, who recorded the ensuing events in one of the finest descriptions of a storm at sea ever written.

'The *Niagara*,' (he writes), 'which had hitherto kept close, whilst the other smaller vessels had dropped out of sight, began to give us a very wide berth, and as darkness increased it was a case of everyone for themselves.

'Our ship, the *Agamemnon*, rolling many degrees—not everyone can imagine how she went it that night—was labouring so heavily she looked like breaking up.

'The massive beams under her upper deck coil (of cable) cracked and snapped with a noise resembling that of small artillery, almost drowning the hideous roar of the wind as it moaned and howled through the rigging, jerking and straining the little storm-sails as though it meant to tear them from the yards. Those in the impoverished cabins of the main deck had little sleep that night, for the upper deck planks above them were "working themselves free" as the sailors say; and beyond a doubt they were infinitely more free than easy, for they groaned under the pressure of the coil with a dreadful uproar, and availed themselves of the opportunity to let in a little light, with a good deal of water at every roll. The sea, too, kept striking with dull, heavy, violence against the vessel's bows, forcing its way through hawse-holes and ill-closed ports with a heavy slush; and thence, hissing and winding aft, it aroused the inhabitants of the cabins aforesaid to the knowledge that their floors were under water, and that the flotsam and jetsam noises they heard beneath were only caused by their outfit for the voyage taking a cruise of its own in some five or six inches of dirty bilge. Such was Sunday night and such was a fair average of all the nights throughout the week, varying only from bad to worse.'

On the second day the storm grew worse. In the words of *The Times* correspondent again, 'about half-past ten o'clock, three or four gigantic waves were seen approaching the ship, coming slowly on through the mist nearer and nearer, rolling on like hills of green water, with a crown of foam that seemed to double their height. The *Agamemnon* rose heavily to the first, and then went down quickly into the deep trough of the sea, falling over as she did so, so as almost to capsize completely on the port side. There was a fearful crashing as she lay over this way, for everything broke adrift, whether secured or not, and the uproar and confusion was terrific for a minute. Then back she came again on the starboard beam in the same manner only quicker, and still deeper than before. Again there was the same noise and crashing, and the officers in the wardroom, who knew the danger of the ship, struggled to their feet and opened the door leading to the main deck. Here, for an instant, the scene almost defies description. Amid loud shouts and efforts to save themselves, a confused mass of sailors, boys, and marines with deck buckets, ropes, ladders, and everything that could get loose, and which had fallen back again to the port side, were being hurled in a mass across the ship to starboard. Dimly, and only for an instant, could this be seen, with groups of men clinging to the beams with all their might, with a mass of water which had forced its way in through ports and decks, surging about; and then with a tremendous crash as the ship fell still deeper over, the coals stowed on the main deck broke loose, and smashing everything before them went over amongst the rest to leeward. The coal-dust hid everything on the main deck in an instant, but the crashing could still be heard going on in all directions as the lumps and sacks of coal, with stanchions, ladders and mess-tins went leaping about the decks, pouring down the hatchways and crashing through the glass skylights into the engine-room below. Still it was not done, and surging again over another tremendous wave, the *Agamemnon* dropped down still more to port, and the coals on the starboard side of the lower deck gave way also, and carried everything before them. Matters now became serious for it was evident that two or three more lurches and the masts would go like reeds, while half the crew might be maimed or killed below. Captain Preedy was already on the poop with Lieutenant Gibson and it was "Hands wear ship" at once, while Mr. Brown, the indefatigable chief engineer, was ordered to get up steam immediately.

'As soon as the *Agamemnon* had gone round on the other tack the *Niagara* wore also, and bore down as if to render assistance. She had witnessed our danger, and as we afterwards learnt, imagined that the upper deck coil had broken loose, and that we were sinking. Things, however, were not so bad as that though they were bad enough, heaven knows, for everything seemed to go wrong that day.'

Eventually *Agamemnon* had to turn and run before the storm. For six days it blew, but all bad things, like all good things, come to an end, and she finished up 200 miles south, battered but still intact. She turned and steamed back to the rendezvous, while the dreadful shambles on board was straightened out. Forty-five members of the crew had been injured, including some seriously hurt when they had been buried by the shifting coal, and some of the cooks who had been scalded by soup from the galley coppers pouring over them. The coil of cable on the main deck had come loose and twisted itself into a wild tangle, which took days to straighten out, while every part of the ship's decks was covered with a sediment of damp coal dust.

At last, on June 26th, *Agamemnon* and *Niagara*, with their escort vessels, met at the mid-ocean rendezvous. The sea was by now 'as calm as Plymouth Sound' and boats were able to pass to and fro between ships, carrying their officers who compared notes on their experiences while arranging the details of the splicing of the two cables. This presented some difficulty, for as already mentioned the two halves had been made with the armouring of each laid in a different direction. It would have been impossible to splice them normally, and, so, to prevent the unwinding of the armouring wires the joint was enclosed in a large wooden casing consisting of two slabs hollowed out to take the cable and bolted together. Iron weights were attached and then the whole contrivance was lowered to the sea-bed while each ship paid out cable. This evolution completed, the ships steamed apart, but only for five miles, when the cable broke on board *Niagara*. A fresh splice was made, but this time a fault developed after forty miles had been laid, and once again the ships had to return to the rendezvous. A third attempt was made, but when some two hundred miles had been laid the cable broke again, this time on board *Agamemnon*. It had been arranged that should a fault occur after each vessel had laid an hundred miles, the ships would return to Queenstown. *Agamemnon* tried to intercept *Niagara*, but without success, and as her coal was running out and the weather was worsening, she turned and made for Ireland.

The confidence of the promoters was by now rather shaken, especially in view of the second failure which had occurred suddenly although the cable was still intact at each ship. Whatever the cause, the fault had occurred at a point on the sea-bottom. Were there unknown hazards on the sea-bed that the surveys had failed to disclose? There had also been a number of mysterious faults and interruptions in the signals between the ships which did nothing to increase their confidence. However, they could not give up now, and so, in mid-July the convoy, having coaled and victualled, set sail from Queenstown once more. The splice was made in mid-Atlantic on July 29th and this time all went well. After an almost uneventful voyage *Niagara* landed her end of the cable at Bay Bulls Arm in Trinity Bay on August 5th, 1858. *Agamemnon* was not quite so lucky, as she encountered another gale and the cable was in danger of breaking. On board her was *The Times* correspondent, who described the journey as follows:

'The day was beautifully calm, so no time was lost before making the splice in latitude 52° 9′ N, longitude 32° 27′ W and soundings of 1500 fathoms. Boats were soon lowered from the attendant ships; the two vessels made fast by a hawser, and *Niagara's* end of the cable conveyed on board *Agamemnon*. About half-past twelve o'clock the splice was effectually made, but with a very different frame from the carefully rounded semi-circular boards which had been used to enclose the junction on previous occasions. It consisted merely of two straight boards hauled over the joint and splice, with the iron rod and leaden plummet attached to the centre. In hoisting it out from the side of the ship, however, the leaden sinker broke short off and fell overboard. There being no more convenient weight at hand a 32 lb. shot was fastened to the splice instead—and the whole apparatus was quickly dropped into the sea without any formality—and almost without a spectator—for those on board the ship had witnessed so many beginnings to the telegraphic line that it was evident that they despaired of there ever being an end to it.

'The stipulated 210 fathoms of cable having been paid out to allow the splice to sink well below the surface, the signal to start was hoisted, the hawser cut loose, and the *Niagara* and the *Agamemnon* started for the last time at about one p.m. for their opposite destinations. . . .

'For the first three hours the ships proceeded very slowly, paying out a great quantity of slack, but after the expiration of this time the speed of the *Agamemnon* was increased to about five knots, the cable going at six, without indicating more than a few hundred pounds of strain on the dynamometer.

'Shortly after four o'clock a very large whale was seen approaching the starboard bow at a great speed, rolling and tossing the sea into foam all around; and for the first time we felt a possibility for the supposition that our second mysterious breakage of the cable might have been caused after all by one of these animals getting foul of it under water. It appeared as if it were making direct for the cable; and great was the relief of all when the ponderous living mass was seen slowly to pass astern, just grazing the cable where it entered the water—but fortunately without doing any mischief. All seemed to go well up to about eight o'clock; the cable paid out from the hold with an evenness and regularity which showed how carefully and perfectly it had been stowed away. The paying-out machinery also worked so smoothly that it left nothing to be desired. . . . Thus far everything looked promising.

'But in such hazardous work no one knows what a few minutes may bring forth, for soon after eight o'clock an injured portion of the cable was discovered about a mile or two from the portion paying out. Not a moment was lost by Mr Canning, the engineer on duty, in setting men to work to cobble up the injury as well as time would permit, for the cable was going out at such a rate that the damaged portion would be paid overboard in less than twenty minutes, and former experience had shown us that to check either the speed of the ship or the cable would in all probability be attended by fatal results. Just before the lapping was finished, Professor Thompson reported that the electrical continuity of the wire had ceased, but that the insulation was still perfect. Attention was naturally directed to the injured piece as the probable source of the stoppage, and not a moment was lost in cutting the cable at that point with the intention of making a perfect splice.

'To the consternation of all, the electrical tests applied showed the fault to be overboard, and in all probability some fifty miles from the ship.

'Not a second was to be lost, for it was evident the cut portion must be paid overboard in a few minutes; and in the meantime the tedious and difficult operation of making a splice had to be performed. The ship was immediately stopped and no more cable paid out than was absolutely necessary to prevent it breaking. As the stern of the ship was lifted by the waves a scene of the most intense excitement followed. It seemed impossible, even by using the greatest possible speed, and paying out the least possible amount of cable, that the junction could be finished before the part was taken out of the hands of the workmen. The main hold presented an extraordinary scene. Nearly all the officers of the ship and those connected with the expedition stood in groups about the coil, watching with intense anxiety as it slowly unwound itself nearer and nearer the joint, while the workmen worked at the splice as only men could work who felt that the life and death of the expedition depended on their rapidity. But all their speed was to no purpose, as the cable was unwinding within a hundred fathoms; and, as a last resort, the cable was stopped altogether, and for a few minutes the ship hung on by the end. Fortunately, however, it was only for a few minutes, as the strain was continually rising above two tons and it would not hold on much longer. When the splice was finished the signal was made to loose the stoppers, and it passed overboard in safety.

'When the excitement had passed away we woke to the consciousness that the case was as hopeless as ever, for the electrical continuity was still entirely wanting.

'Preparations were consequently made to pay out as little cable as possible, and to hold on for six hours in the hope that the fault, whatever it was, might mend itself, before cutting the cable and returning to the rendezvous to make another splice. The magnetic needles on the receiving instruments were watched closely for the returning signals, when, in a few minutes, the last hope was extinguished by their suddenly indicating dead earth, which tended to show that the cable had broken from the *Niagara* or that the insulation had been completely destroyed.

'Nothing however could be done. The only course was to wait until the current should return or take its final departure. And it *did* return—with greater strength than ever—for in three minutes everyone was agreeably surprised by the intelligence that the stoppage had disappeared and that the signals had again appeared at their regular intervals from the *Niagara*.* It is needless to say what a load of anxiety this removed from the minds of everyone, but the general confidence in the ultimate success of the operations was much shaken by the occurrence, for all felt that every minute a similar accident might occur.

'For some time the paying out continued as usual, but towards the morning another damaged place was discovered in the cable. There was fortunately time, however, to repair it in the hold without

---

* Later on it was made clear that this mysterious temporary want of continuity . . . was due to a defect in the more or less inconstant sand battery used aboard the latter vessel.

in any way interfering with the operations, beyond for a time reducing the speed of the ship. During the morning of Friday the 30th, everything went well. The ship had been kept at a speed of about five knots, the cable going out at six, the average angle with the horizon at which it left the ship being about 15°, while the indicated strain upon the dynamometer seldom exceeded 1600 lbs. to 1700 lbs.'

The *Agamemnon* seemed to be dogged by bad weather, however. On this same day, towards evening, the barometer started to drop, and when darkness fell the ship was steaming at full power into the teeth of a gale. Topmasts, spars, sails, and everything aloft that could be lowered was sent down to decrease resistance to the wind. Coal supplies were being rapidly exhausted as the boilers were put on to forced draught to maintain speed.* It was ironic that on the outward journey they had been forced to use up coal because of a lack of wind; now they were suffering for the very opposite reason.

On Saturday the wind veered round to the south-west, thus enabling them to husband their small remaining store of fuel, but the gale still blew as fiercely as ever. This is how *The Times* reporter described the scene:

'Now, indeed, were the energy and activity of all engaged in the operation taxed to the utmost. Mr. Hoar and Mr. Moore—the two engineers who had charge of the relieving wheels of the dynamometer —had to keep watch and watch alternately every four hours, and while on duty durst not let their attention be removed from their occupation for one moment; for on their releasing the brakes every time the stern of the ship fell into the trough of the sea entirely depended the safety of the cable, and the result shows how ably they discharged their duty.

'Throughout the night there were few who had the least expectation of the cable holding on till morning, and many lay awake listening for the sound that all most dreaded to hear—the sound of the gun which should announce the failure of all our hopes. But still the cable—which in comparison with the ship from which it was paid out, and the gigantic waves among which it was delivered, was but a mere thread—continued to hold on, only leaving a silvery

---

* The *Agamemnon* was fitted up so that forced draught could be used for short periods to 'boost' the indicated horse power to 900.

phosphorous line upon the stupendous seas as they rolled on towards the ship. . . .

'At noon on Monday August the 2nd, observations showed us to be in lat. 52° 35' N, long 19° 48' W. Thus we had made good 127½ miles since noon of the previous day and had completed more than half way to our ultimate destination.

'During the afternoon an American three-masted schooner, which afterwards proved to be the *Chieftain*, was seen standing from the eastward towards us. No notice was taken of her at first, but when she was within about half a mile of *Agamemnon*, she altered her course and bore right down across our bows. A collision which might prove fatal to the cable now seemed inevitable; or could only have been avoided by the equally hazardous expedient of altering *Agamemnon's* course. The *Valorous* steamed ahead and fired a gun for her to heave to, which, as she did not appear to take much notice of it, was quickly followed by another from the bows of *Agamemnon* and a second and third from *Valorous*. But still the vessel held on her course; and, as the only resource left to avoid a collision, the course of the *Agamemnon* was altered just in time to pass within a few yards of her. It was evident that our proceedings were a source of the greatest possible astonishment to them, for all her crew crowded upon her deck and rigging. At length they evidently discovered what we were doing and who we were, for the crew manned the riggings, and, dipping the ensign several times, they gave us three hearty cheers. Though the *Agamemnon* was obliged to answer these congratulations in due form, the feeling of annoyance with which we regarded the vessel—which (either by the stupidity or carelessness of those on board) was so near adding a fatal and unexpected mishap to the long chapter of accidents which had already been encountered —may easily be imagined.

'To those below—who of course did not see the ship approaching— the sound of the first gun came like a thunderbolt, for all took it to be a signal of the breaking of the cable. The dinner tables were deserted in a moment, and a general rush made up the hatches to the deck; but before reaching it their fears were quickly banished by the report of the succeeding gun, which all knew could only be caused by a ship in our way, or a man overboard.'

After whales, storms, and imminent collisions, one might have thought that *Agamemnon's* dangers would be over. But more was to follow, for at three o'clock in the grey light of Tuesday morning another signal gun brought our correspondent from his bed just in time to see another American vessel, a barque, about to cross the stern of the cable-layer right through the precious cable. The attendant *Valorous* was, however, able to put herself between the two vessels, firing gun after gun in quick succession until the barque threw her sails aback and hove to. The cable fleet moved on, leaving an astonished sailing vessel crew wondering at this outrage on the American flag.

Wednesday was a beautiful, calm day; the water had shallowed to 200 fathoms by the evening and everyone felt that the worst was over. At the other end of the cable *Niagara* also reported 200 fathoms as she steamed over the Newfoundland Banks, and it was felt that success was near. It is interesting to note that throughout the voyage *Agamemnon* and *Niagara* were in constant communication with each other, signals being sent through the cable at ten-minute intervals. Not for nearly half a century, when ships were fitted with wireless telegraphy, would it be possible again for two ships to keep in touch with each other all the way across the Atlantic.

At about midnight on Wednesday the Skelligs Light was seen in the distance, and speed was reduced so as not to arrive before daylight, and on the following day land was reached. *The Times* described the end of the venture.

'By daylight on the morning of Thursday the 5th August, the bold and rocky mountains which entirely surround the wild and picturesque neighbourhood of Valentia rose right before us at a few miles distance. Never, probably, was the sight of land more welcome, as it brought to a successful conclusion one of the greatest, but at the same time most difficult schemes which was ever undertaken. Had it been the dullest and most melancholy swamp on the face of the earth that lay before us, we should have found it a pleasant prospect; but as the sun rose behind the estuary of Dingle bay, tingeing with a soft deep purple the lofty summits of the steep mountains which surround its shores, illuminating the masses of morning vapour which hung upon them, it was a scene which might vie in beauty with anything that could be produced by the most florid imagination of an artist.

'No one on shore was apparently conscious of our approach, so the *Valorous* went ahead to the mouth of the harbour and fired a gun. Both ships made straight for Doulas Bay, the *Agamemnon* steaming into the harbour with a feeling that she had done something, and about 6 a.m. came to anchor at the side of Beginish Island, opposite to Valentia.

'As soon as the inhabitants became aware of our approach there was a general desertion of the place, and hundreds of boats crowded round us—their passengers in the greatest state of excitement to hear all about our voyage. The Knight of Kerry was absent in Dingle, but a messenger was immediately despatched for him, and he soon arrived in Her Majesty's gunboat *Shamrock*.

'Soon after our arrival a signal was received from the *Niagara* that they were preparing to land, having paid out 1030 nautical miles of cable, while the *Agamemnon* had accomplished her portion of the distance with an expenditure of 1020 miles, making a total length of wire submerged of 2050 miles.

'Immediately after the ships cast anchor, the paddlebox boats of the *Valorous* were got ready, and two miles of cable coiled in them, for the purpose of landing the end. But it was late in the afternoon before the procession of boats left the ship, to the salute of three rounds of small arms from the detachment of Royal Marines on board the *Agamemnon*, under the command of Lieutenant Morris.

'The progress of the end to shore was slow, in consequence of the stiff wind which blew at the time; but at about 3 p.m. the end was safely brought on shore at Knightstown, Valentia, by Mr. Bright, to whose exertions the success of the undertaking is attributable. Mr. Bright was accompanied by Mr. Canning and the Knight of Kerry. The end was immediately laid in the trench which had been dug to receive it; while a royal salute, making the neighbouring rocks and mountains reverberate, announced that the communication between the Old and New World had been completed.

'The cable was taken into the electrical room by Mr. Whitehouse and attached to a galvanometer, and the first message was received through the entire length now lying on the bed of the sea.'

The temporary station which had been set up close to the edge of the cliffs was housed in what a newspaper reporter described as a 'Crimean hut' (ex-army surplus?), built of wood and well covered in pitch. From the entrance at one end a corridor led down the middle of the hut, with rooms on either side of it in which the telegraph clerks had their quarters. At the end of the corridor, and occupying the width of the hut, was the 'electrical room'. Along its far end was a narrow bench, below which were the Mennotti cells which provided the power. On the bench, at the seaward end, were the submarine cable instruments; mirror galvanometers to receive and double keys for sending (one key for a dot and the other for a dash). The cable itself came into the building and terminated close to the instruments; that line the other end of which rose out of the waters of Trinity Bay, Newfoundland. At the other end of the bench were the Wheatstone and Cooke magnetic telegraph instruments which were connected by an ordinary air-line carried on poles with the telegraph station at Valentia. Such was the building from which passed the first telegraph messages from the Old World to the New.

In contrast to *Agamemnon*, *Niagara* had an uneventful passage. Apart from meeting some icebergs towards the end of the voyage, nothing of moment was reported. On the evening of August 4th she was approaching Trinity Bay with her escort vessel, H.M.S. *Gorgon*. Awaiting their arrival in the bay was H.M.S. *Porcupine*, which had gone out a month before to survey a deep channel to the telegraph station at Bull Arm. Bull Arm is an inlet at the head of Trinity Bay, chosen because of its deep water and sheltered position. Here *Porcupine* and her crew waited for the cable layer. Trinity Bay is an arm of the sea, some eighty miles in length, and near Bull Arm, on a high point overlooking the bay which is now known as Niagara Point, Captain Otter of *Porcupine* had established a look-out post. From here the watchers were able to sight the *Niagara* when she was still forty miles away, and pass the news on to *Porcupine* by lighting a beacon fire. At 7.0 p.m. H.M.S. *Porcupine* met the telegraph ships, and Captain Otter went aboard U.S.S. *Niagara*. The convoy proceeded, *Porcupine* leading, followed by *Gorgon* and then *Niagara*. Near Bull Arm, Captain Otter had a number of small boats lining the sides of the channel, and as the ships approached the boats lit blue flares and then hoisted a lantern each. On the hills overlooking the harbour, which were covered with pine trees, the beacon fire had spread to the surrounding woods, and the whole area was illuminated as if to celebrate the historic occasion. To the local inhabitants who had turned out to watch, it must have presented an unforgettable spectacle. At about 1 a.m. those on shore heard the rattle of chains as the ships anchored, and *Niagara's* work was completed.

At 8.45 a.m. the boats left for the shore with the end of the cable. A pathway had been cut through the trees, and up this the cable was carried with the willing help of the onlookers who had collected. One eye-witness stated that 'even ladies wearing white gloves' laid hold of the precious wire. Some six hundred yards from the beach a terminal hut had been erected and in this the submarine cable was joined up to the aerial line which was carried on poles to the telegraph station two miles away. Before this was done however, some test instruments were connected up to the cable in the terminal hut, and shortly afterwards Cyrus Field came out, and standing among the tree stumps announced to the waiting crowd that they had made contact with Valentia and that very strong currents of electricity had been received through the whole cable from the other side of the Atlantic. Captain Hudson of *Niagara* then asked those present to join with him in a prayer of thanksgiving to Almighty God for the successful conclusion of the enterprise. He might well have echoed the words of another seaman of other days, Sir Francis Drake, who prayed 'O Lord, when thou givest to Thy servants to endeavour any great matter, grant us also to know that it is not the beginning, but the continuing of the same until it be thoroughly finished, which yieldeth the true glory'.

On August 8th the three ships sailed for St. John's. They remained there till the 11th, taking part in the general festivities which included a parade, illuminations, a grand ball, and a regatta. The regatta, held at the beginning of August every year, is still one of the big events in the social life of St. John's. A public holiday is declared, and crowds from all around St. John's flock to the shores of Quidi Vidi Lake, just outside the city, where the races are held in an atmosphere of Derby Day in England, with booths, sideshows, refreshment tents and all the fun of the fair. The 1858 regatta, at which the crews of the cable ships were the guests of honour, was no doubt even more of a celebration than usual, with spruce beer and 'Screech' (a liquor peculiar to Newfoundland) flowing freely. Newfoundlanders are hospitable people, and never reluctant to celebrate a good cause.

The news that the cable had been successfully laid was greeted with tremendous enthusiasm on both sides of the Atlantic. In New York there were torchlight processions, City Hall was illuminated (and caught fire in the process), and congratulations poured in. In England it was announced that the honour of knighthood had been conferred on Mr. Charles Bright at the early age of 26, and messages were exchanged between Queen Victoria and the President of the United States via the cable. Unfortunately it took ten hours for the Queen's message to reach Washington; the cable from Newfoundland to the mainland had been allowed to get out of order, and to begin with all messages had to be carried across the straits by the company's steamship, *Victoria*.

Even when the cable had been repaired, however, communication was still slow. There appeared to be some difficulty in getting the line working. To begin with the Atlantic Telegraph Company announced that it would be about three weeks before they would be able to accept messages from the public. For days after the cable had been laid, the only notices that appeared in the London newspapers were to the effect that 'the instruments at each end of the cable were in process of being adjusted'. In actual fact, what was happening was a trial of strength between the representatives of two different schools of thought among the technicians concerned in the enterprise. On the one hand Dr. Whitehouse wanted to use for a receiver his own magnetic recorder, an instrument which required a strong current to operate it. This current could only be achieved over the great distance involved by using a very high voltage. On the other hand Professor Thompson took the view that the cable could be worked with comparatively small currents by using his very sensitive mirror galvanometer. First one instrument was used, then the other. After each time the high voltage was applied it became obvious that the cable insulation was less effective, and messages were passed only with difficulty, and with frequent repetitions. In addition, each message between London and New York had to be manually relayed six times.

The telegraph station at Valentia has already been described. The one at Bull Arm was similar, but bigger and consisting of two storeys. The telegraph wires entered through one of the downstairs windows. The instrument room was fitted up as at Valentia. Inside it telegraph clerks operated Professor Thompson's specially designed instruments. The Wheatstone receiver, as used on the inland telegraphs, was no use for signals received over the great distance required, and so Professor Thompson had evolved the mirror galvanometer in time for the 1857 expedition. Instruments of this type had been in use on board the cable-laying ships and were now moved ashore. They consisted of a tiny mirror to which was attached a bar magnet, and which was suspended by a silk thread in the centre of a coil of fine wire. This coil was connected at one end to the cable, and at the other to earth, so that every time a signal was received through the cable an electric current passed through the coil, causing the magnet and the mirror to move slightly. This deflection of the mirror was magnified by a beam of light from an oil-lamp which shone through an aperture on to the mirror and was reflected on to a scale. As the mirror was moved by a signal, the reflected beam of light moved to right or left, representing a dot or dash respectively in the Morse Code. One clerk (known as the mirror clerk) watched the beam of light and read off the signals while another clerk wrote them down. The mirror clerk's job was a very exacting one, and required a good deal of training.

For sending messages a double sending key was employed, one key for dots and the other for dashes. Power was supplied by a battery of twenty Menotti cells, the voltage being increased by an induction coil.

When work first commenced on the Atlantic cable little or nothing was known of the effects of inductance or capacity in a long length of cable. The uninsulated 'airline' wires carried on poles over land were not subject to these phenomena to any appreciable extent, but the submarine cable with its armoured covering was, in effect, a huge condenser. After a few signals the cable became charged, and it was necessary to wait for the charge to leak away before another signal could be sent. Consequently at its opening, the cable was only able to pass signals at the rate of fifteen letters per minute—well below the reading capacity of a mirror-clerk. The first attempt to overcome this difficulty was the use of a special sending key by means of which every electrical impulse through the cable was followed by an immediate and similar one in the opposite direction to cancel out the effects of the first. Not until some time later was it realised that the capacitance of the cable could be reduced by increasing its inductance.

The first public message to pass through the Atlantic cable was sent on August 17th, twelve days after the cable had been completed. It consisted of a message for the Cunard Shipping Line, giving information of a collision at sea between the S.S. *Arabia* and S.S. *Europa*, both ships having put into St. John's. The latter half of the message read 'no lives lost will you do it stay anxiety non-arrival' and no words could better illustrate the tremendous effect of the submarine telegraph on people's lives. Previously, the ships concerned would have been posted as overdue and days of anxiety would have followed until news of them was received.

The rate charged at this time was $100 (£22) for a minimum of twenty words. It is worth noting that today the rate for the same service is eightpence per word, a direct reflection of the extent to which traffic over cables has been speeded up.

Unfortunately, the triumph of the Atlantic Telegraph Company was short-lived. From the very first message the cable proved unreliable, and much repetition of messages was necessary. It was soon obvious that the insulation was impaired, and as August passed signals became more and more unintelligible. By September only a few words could be transmitted at intervals, and by October 20th the cable went completely dead. All further attempts to bring it to life were useless.

The reasons for this have never been fully explained, though when one considers it, the wonder is not that it failed, but that it ever worked at all. The cable was manufactured in a hurry, without any previous experience to draw upon, and with no time for experiment. Parts of it had been out of the water for over a year. It had been coiled and uncoiled as many as ten times, and between the 1857 and 1858 expeditions it had been standing on the dockside at Keyham. It was later found that it had been exposed to the sun which had probably softened the gutta-percha and allowed the central conductor to become displaced. Finally, there was the frightful tangle into which the main deck coil had got on board *Agamemnon* during the great storm. Any of these might have provided a good reason for the cable's failure, but there is little doubt that the *coup de grâce* was administered by the company's own Chief Electrician, Dr. Whitehouse. William Wildman Whitehouse was a physician by profession and an amateur electrician. Although highly thought of as an authority on electrical theory, he had little practical experience, and disagreed on many points with his assistant, de Sauty. As already mentioned, one of the difficulties encountered in working the cable was the effect of the capacitance which seriously delayed transmissions. Whitehouse's answer to this was the answer of brute force rather than of brains, and hardly what one would have expected from an expert in electrical theory. He attempted to overcome the cable's capacitance by increasing the voltage of the signals. For this purpose he had assembled a battery of 500 voltaic cells. Not content with this formidable array, he added a huge five-foot long induction coil which he had constructed. What the ensuing potential was is not recorded, and probably not even Whitehouse himself knew, but when it was applied to the long-suffering cable the effect on the insulation, already damaged, was disastrous. After every application of Whitehouse's apparatus, the signals received by normal means were weaker, and there is little doubt that he eventually succeeded in destroying the insulation completely.

Following the failure of the cable he was recalled to England by the company and dismissed from their service. He protested that he was being made a scapegoat for the failure of the enterprise, and later published a pamphlet in which he attempted to justify his actions. There is little doubt, however, that he was responsible for hastening the cable's untimely end.

So ended the first attempt to bridge the Atlantic by telegraph. Although it had been a failure commercially, it had demonstrated that Cyrus Field's scheme was practicable once the initial difficulties had been overcome. It had added tremendously to men's knowledge and experience of submarine telegraphy and paved the way for later successful efforts. The achievements of those responsible for laying the 1858 cable have been overshadowed by the fame accorded to the later, and more successful, endeavour of 1866. Indeed, the 1866 cable is often referred to as the first Atlantic cable. When one considers, however, the tremendous difficulties encountered by the first expedition; the kind of ships they had to use, the primitive methods of handling the cable and the unknown hazards they faced, one is filled with admiration for their courage and pertinacity. Thanks to their efforts the next Atlantic cable was laid under far easier conditions.

However, the Atlantic Telegraph Company had to face the fact that they had lost a further £500,000 of capital. The return they had received from it had so far been small. It consisted of the receipts from August 17th to October 20th plus what the enterprising Cyrus Field had made by selling the surplus cable to the well-known firm of New York jewellers, Tiffanys, who cut it into short lengths of about six inches, mounted them in silver, and sold them as souvenirs of the occasion with a facsimile of a certificate signed by Field as proof of their origin. The company did not feel disposed to make another attempt in spite of all that Field could do to try to persuade them.

The failure in 1859 of the Red Sea cable which had cost some £800,000 discouraged investors still further from putting their money into submarine cables, and finally the outbreak of the American Civil War in the spring of 1861 put an end for the time being to any thought of a new attempt. The *Niagara* reverted to her role of warship and played a prominent part in the struggle on the side of the Union, while relations between Britain and the Union were strained over the question of the *Alabama*, and any idea of Anglo–American co-operation in cable laying became out of the question. To Cyrus Field, however, all these things were simply set-backs, delaying the time when his grand project should be completed. Meanwhile, he must be content with his telegraph to Cape Race, where John Murphy's boat continued to hail the passing steamers and the tin-can mail maintained the link between America and Europe.

CHAPTER 3

The Great Eastern's *Cable, 1865*

FOUR YEARS PASSED without any further move by the Atlantic Telegraph Company, for the reasons which have already been mentioned. Though its cable was useless the company was kept in being against the day when work could begin again; and while the general public, and especially investors, had lost interest in the venture, Cyrus Field never gave up hope. He had the British Government, too, on his side, for the British Empire was growing, the red areas on the map of the world were multiplying, and the value of the submarine telegraph in maintaining communications with the homeland was obvious. So in 1860, two years after the failure of the Atlantic cable, a select committee was set up by the Privy Council to enquire into and report upon the whole field of submarine telegraphy. The chairman was Captain (later Sir) Douglas Galton, Royal Engineers, and the other members consisted of Professor Wheatstone, one of the pioneers of telegraphy; George P. Bidder, a noted railway engineer; the brothers Edwin and Latimer Clarke, who with Sir Charles Bright were later responsible for the invention of the system of electrical units in use today; William Fairbairn; George Saward; and Cromwell Varley. In two years the committee held 22 sittings, and questioned engineers, electricians, physicists, manufacturers and seamen; in fact representatives of all those who had had any experience in the various branches of cable work. Those cables already laid were investigated from the point of view of structure, materials and manufacture. Actual laboratory experiments were conducted in connection with the enquiry to ascertain (*a*) electrical and mechanical qualities of copper, both pure and alloyed, and also of gutta percha and other insulating substances; (*b*) the chemical change in their condition when submerged; (*c*) the effect of temperature and pressure on the insulator; (*d*) the elongation and breaking strain of copper wires and of iron, steel and tarred hemp separately and combined; (*e*) the phenomena connected with electrically charging and discharging conductors; (f) the methods of testing conductors and of locating faults.

The report, which was finally published after three years, constitutes an invaluable record of the state of scientific knowledge of this subject at the time. There is no doubt that if the enquiry had taken place before the first Atlantic cable was laid most of the mistakes made would have been avoided. Indeed, the committee made this point in their report, which ended with the following statement.

'London, 13th July, 1863.

'We, the undersigned, members of the committee who were appointed by the Board of Trade in 1859 to investigate the question of submarine telegraphy, do hereby state as the result of our deliberations that a well-insulated cable, properly protected, of suitable specific gravity, made with care and tested under water throughout its progress with the best-known apparatus, and paid into the ocean with the most improved machinery, possesses every prospect of not only being successfully laid in the first instance, but may reasonably be relied upon to continue for many years in an efficient state for the transmission of signals.'

The report was a great encouragement to Field. For the last year he had been trying to raise the capital required to manufacture and lay a new cable. This, it was estimated, would cost £600,000, and so far, try as he might, he had only succeeded after tremendous efforts, in raising £285,000. America was in the throes of a civil war and capital was hard to find; he must therefore look to Britain for the necessary money, and the report, he hoped, would make this easier.

Another encouraging feature was the success of the first cable to India laid, in several sections, by Sir Charles Bright in 1863 and 1864.

This had shown several advances in technique; advances in electrical and mechanical testing of the cable; the use of Chatterton's compound to seal the gutta percha insulation to the conductor, and treatment of the iron armouring to prevent corrosion. Further experience in cable-laying had moved the art out of the realms of pioneering and into the field of routine application. Altogether, the prospects for a new attempt on the Atlantic telegraph seemed much brighter.

And this indeed was the case, for early in 1864 Field, on one of his many visits to England, met Thomas Brassey, son of the great civil engineering contractor and builder of railways in every part of the globe. Brassey was full of encouragement and suggested an approach to Glass, Elliot & Co., the cable makers, to see if they would lay as well as manufacture the cable. As a result of this, Glass, Elliot & Co., and the Gutta Percha Company, who had also been concerned in the manufacture of previous cables, now decided to unite in one single company, to carry on the manufacture and laying of submarine cables. On April 7th, 1864, the new company was formally registered as The Telegraph Construction and Maintenance Company with an authorised capital of £1,000,000. The first action of its directors was to approach the Atlantic Telegraph Company with an offer to subscribe the remaining £315,000 of capital required in return for the contract to manufacture and lay the Atlantic cable. Needless to say, the offer was accepted, and once more work began on another project.

This time, profiting from previous experience and the report of the Committee of Enquiry, much more care was given to the design of the cable, and manufacture was only commenced after considerable experiment and investigation. The core of the cable was three times the size of the old one and consisted of seven strands of No. 18 Birmingham Wire Gauge copper wire set in Chatterton's compound (a mixture of gutta percha and Stockholm tar) and weighing 400 lb. per mile compared with the old cable's 261 lb. It will thus be seen that though three times the volume of the old cable it was less than twice the weight, and in consequence would not sink so rapidly when laid, thus reducing the strain on the cable as it left the ship. In addition, the iron outer covering was of improved quality, with a greater tensile strength. It was due to these facts that the laying of the new cable was to prove much simpler than before.

The core was served with tanned jute yarn and covered with ten ungalvanised soft iron wires of No. 13 B.W.G., each wire being previously compounded and served with five tarred strands of manilla hemp. The total diameter was 1·1 inch, its weight in air 3,930 lb. per mile, and in water 1,568 lb. It had a breaking strain of more than 7 tons. Unlike the previous cables, it was made in one continuous length of 2,300 miles.

And now the question arose of how the cable was to be laid. A ship far bigger than *Agamemnon* or *Niagara* was required, for not only was the cable in one piece, but it occupied far more space than the previous ones. But by a fortunate coincidence of history such a ship now existed. It is always fascinating to observe, in studying economic history, how often one scientific advance has depended on another taking place at the same time; for example James Watt's improvement to the steam engine provided power for pumping water which made deep coal mining possible for the first time, and this in turn provided the necessary fuel to enable the new steam power to be applied to industry. So it was with the submarine cable. While the necessary progress had been made in developing the telegraphic apparatus, a tremendous leap forward in the science of shipbuilding had produced the right vessel to lay the cable.

The ship was the *Great Eastern*, the creation of Isambard Kingdom Brunel, engineer of the Great Western Railway, builder of great bridges, and designer of the first iron ship and the first screw-propelled ship to cross the Atlantic. Among the engineering giants of the nineteenth century Brunel stands out as perhaps the greatest. All his designs were on a heroic scale, such as the Great Western Railway which he built to the broad gauge of 7 feet rather than the standard gauge of 4 feet $8\frac{1}{2}$ inches with which other engineers were content. The *Great Eastern* was no exception to this rule. In all the history of naval architecture she was probably the most ambitious failure. Six times the size of any ship then afloat, it was forty years before the world saw her like. She had been intended by her designer for the Indian and Australian trade. The discovery of gold in Australia in 1851 had started a wave of emigration and a boom in the shipping trade, which gave Brunel his cue. His last design had been the *Great Western*, built for the New York run, and therefore, in view of her destination, it was natural that his new ship should be called *Great Eastern*. In actual fact the name she was formally given on launching (accompanied by the usual bottle of champagne) was *Leviathan*, and she was also referred to as *The Great Ship* or *The Great Iron Ship*. For purposes of registration, however, she was always *Great Eastern*.

By the standards of her time she was truly gigantic. Her length was 692 feet, her breadth 82·7 feet, and her draught reached 30 feet. She displaced 32,000 tons. There were three distinct methods of propulsion. Firstly, she was rigged as a sailing ship with six masts, all carrying fore-and-aft sails. In addition the two foremost masts were square-rigged giving a total sail area of 6,500 square feet. Secondly, she was fitted with a pair of steam-powered paddle wheels, each 56 feet in diameter. They were driven by four huge oscillating cylinders 6 feet 2 inches in diameter by 14 feet stroke, working at a pressure of 24 lb. per square inch. These gave an indicated horsepower of 3,410 and working on their own could propel *Great Eastern* at seven and a quarter knots. Thirdly, a screw propeller 24 feet in diameter and of 37 feet pitch was driven by engines constructed by Messrs. James Watt and Co. of Birmingham which had four horizontal direct-acting cylinders 7 feet in diameter by 4 feet stroke. At 25 lb. per square inch pressure, these gave an indicated horse power of 4,890. By itself the screw could push the Great Ship along at nine knots, and paddle and screw together gave a speed of fifteen knots.

This unique method of propulsion was chosen to enable the ship to enter the Hooghly River over the bar, where paddles would be better than the screw. It also gave her great manoeuvrability, for she could turn in her own length or go astern on the paddles and ahead on the screw and stand still while still answering to her rudder. This was important, for the harbours and docks of those days were not made for ships the size of *Great Eastern* and she would have to manoeuvre in very restricted conditions. It had the disadvantage of the added complication involving two engine-rooms and two sets of boilers. Her sails were little used; there is only one recorded occasion of them all being set together. She could carry 12,000 tons of coal which she consumed at the rate of over 300 tons a day.

But size was not the only outstanding feature of *Great Eastern* for in her construction she foreshadowed the era of the modern ship. Mr. John Scott Russell, the builder, designed the hull according to his 'wave-line' principle, and at Brunel's request it was of cellular construction. Two skins 2·8 feet apart extended from the keel to the water line and were spaced by webs of iron 6 feet apart. There were four decks and the hull was divided transversely into ten separate watertight compartments, pierced only by two tunnels below the second deck. With her five funnels and six masts, *Great Eastern* when at sea must have provided an unmistakable silhouette.

Brunel died when his great ship was on her maiden voyage, and she was never employed on the trade for which he had designed her. Indeed, had she been, the opening of the Suez Canal in 1869 would have rendered her obsolete, for she was too large to pass through it.

Instead, she was used on the Atlantic route to New York, but was never a commercial success either as a passenger or as a cargo ship. Now in 1865 she was laid up and out of employment. Brunel's prophetic words to Cyrus Field 'There is the ship to lay your Atlantic cable' were about to come true, and when one considers it, what could be more fitting than the joining of these two great enterprises? The history of *Great Eastern* is itself an epic of as great proportions as the story of the Atlantic cable; both stand out with the same grandeur among the technological advances of the nineteenth century.

There can be little doubt that Cyrus Field, when considering the latest attempt to lay an Atlantic cable, must have had in mind the use of *Great Eastern*, as is shown by the decision to make the cable in one length. He had also, it will be remembered, conferred with Thomas Brassey, who was an important shareholder in the firm which owned the ship. It was hardly a coincidence therefore that just before the new cable was ready *Great Eastern* should be put up for auction by her owners.

At the last minute, however, a snag arose. The Atlantic Telegraph Company were unable to raise the additional money required to bid for the great ship and it seemed as though the unique chance might be lost. Fortunately one of the directors of the company was Daniel Gooch, formerly Locomotive Superintendent of the Great Western Railway under Brunel, and later to become its Secretary. With Thomas Brassey and a Mr. Barber he formed a partnership to bid for *Great Eastern*, intending to charter her to the cable company if successful. And so indeed he was, for the partners went to the auction prepared to bid up to £80,000, only to have the great vessel knocked down to them for £25,000, an indication of the number of companies she had bankrupted.

Gooch and his partners now made a sporting offer to the cable-laying contractors, the Telegraph Construction and Maintenance Company. They offered the use of *Great Eastern* to lay the Atlantic cable. If the attempt was successful they were to receive £50,000 in company stock. If it failed, they would receive nothing. And so began the most useful period in the whole career of Brunel's ship. 'The work has the best wishes and prayers of all who know it', Gooch wrote. 'Its success will open out a useful future for our noble ship, lift her out of the depression under which she has laboured from her birth, and satisfy me that I have done wisely in never losing confidence in her; and the world may still feel thankful to my old friend Brunel that he designed and carried out the construction of so noble a work.'

At this point it would perhaps be as well to recall the different business organisations which had by now become involved in this gigantic operation. Firstly, there was Cyrus Field's original creation, the New York, Newfoundland and London Telegraph Company, financed with American capital, registered in Newfoundland, and holding the sole right to land submarine cables in that country. Its overland line extended through Canada and Newfoundland to Cape Race, where it awaited the link with the Atlantic cable. Secondly, there was the Atlantic Telegraph Company, formed by Field mainly with British capital and registered in Britain with the object of laying the submarine cable. Thirdly, there was the newly formed Telegraph Construction and Maintenance Company acting under contract to the Atlantic Telegraph Company for the manufacture and laying of the cable. Finally there were Gooch and his partners, owners of *Great Eastern*, which they had chartered to the Telegraph Construction and Maintenance Company.

To enable *Great Eastern* to lay the cable considerable modifications were necessary. The fourth funnel passed through the main hold, and to enable this to be used the funnel was removed, thus putting out of action the fourth boiler room and altering the famous silhouette. A cable tank was built in the hold, and two others in the fore and after holds. These three tanks would hold the entire 2,300 miles of cable and enable it to be stored under water. From where the cable issued from the main hold a trough carried it aft to the paying-out mechanism. The length of deck along which this trough passed, the busiest part of the ship when laying was in progress, became known to the crew as 'Oxford Street'. At the stern was the paying-out mechanism, much improved on the earlier types, while at the bows was a winch for hauling in cable, worked by its own donkey engine and boiler. The main deck of *Great Eastern* was flush from stem to stern, but had five deck houses at various points. From their likeness to railway coaches, these were known as 'cabooses' and one of them, below the forward flying bridge, was now blacked out and fitted up with a bench for the use of the electricians. When these modifications were complete, *Great Eastern* sailed for Sheerness to take on cable.

This process took no less than five months. The cable was brought down from Greenwich in two old hulks which were moored alongside *Great Eastern* and the cable manhandled on board and coiled down in the tanks. As soon as a tank was filled it was flooded and the cable immersed in water. By the time all the tanks were filled 2,000 tons of water had been pumped in, in addition to 5,000 tons of cable, and to this was added 8,000 tons of coal. Stores included 500 chickens, 120 sheep, 20 pigs and 18,000 eggs.

Commanding *Great Eastern* was Captain Anderson of the Cunard Company. Among those on board were Cyrus Field, Sir Charles Bright, and Daniel Gooch. Professor Thompson and Mr. Varley were present representing the Atlantic Telegraph Company; by the terms of the contract they could give advice (in writing) but could not interfere in any way. They also had to test the cable when laid, and pass it as efficient before it would be accepted from the contractors. Once again the Engineer in charge of the laying was Samuel Canning, and the Chief Electrician Mr. de Sauty.

On Saturday, July 15th, 1865, *Great Eastern* sailed from Sheerness for Ireland. Shortly before her departure the Prince of Wales had come on board to visit. In the electricians' caboose he gave a message. 'I wish success to the Atlantic Cable.' An operator tapped it out on his key and each signal traversed the 2,300 miles of cable in the holds and returned to the caboose in a fraction of a second.

From Sheerness, *Great Eastern* made for Foilhummerum Bay, Valentia, towing behind her the S.S. *Caroline*, a small vessel carrying the length of heavy cable for the shore end. Once again crowds assembled to see the beginning of the great enterprise. They had come also to see the great ship, but in this they were disappointed, for *Great Eastern* could approach no nearer than Bantry Bay on account of her size, and from there she handed her cable end to *Caroline*, who spliced it to her own, and proceeded to lay that inshore. On Sunday, July 23rd, when all was ready, *Great Eastern* weighed anchor and stood out to sea. Accompanying her and acting as escorts were Her Majesty's Ships *Sphinx* and *Terrible*. On board her, in addition to the technicians already mentioned, were Cyrus Field and Daniel Gooch. As historian of the enterprise there was Dr. W. H. Russell, a well-known *Times* correspondent, and Mr.

Robert Dudley, who was the official artist. This is how Dr. Russell described the beginning of the voyage:

'The bight of the cable was slipped from the *Caroline* at 7.15 p.m. and the *Great Eastern* stood slowly on her course N.W. ¼ W. Then the *Terrible* and *Sphinx* which had ranged alongside, and sent their crews into the shrouds and up to the tops to give her a parting cheer, delivered their friendly broadsides with vigour and received a similar greeting. Their colours were hauled down, and as the sun set a broad stream of golden light was thrown across the smooth billows towards their bows as if to indicate and illumine the path marked out by the hand of heaven. The brake was eased, and as the Great Eastern moved ahead the machinery of the paying-out apparatus began to work, drums rolled, wheel whirled, and out spun the black line of the cable, and dropped in a graceful curve into the sea over the stern wheel. The cable came up with ease from the after tank and was paid out with the utmost regularity from the apparatus. The system of signals to and from the ship was at once in play between the electricians on board and those at Foilhummerum.'

In the darkened electricians' caboose a constant watch was kept on the flickering light of the mirror galvanometer. By means of it communication was kept up with the shore end of the cable. News of the cable ship's progress was forwarded regularly to the company in London, and in return news of the outside world was received on board. Long before the days of wireless, *Great Eastern* was the first vessel to cross the Atlantic and keep in constant touch with the outside world. But Professor Thompson's instrument could do more than receive messages in morse. By graduating the scale over which the beam of light moved it was possible to measure the intensity of the electric impulses received, and continuous tests of the cable for conduction and insulation were carried out. Moreover, the Professor's forethought in insisting on a standard purity of copper, and thus a standard value of resistance for the core of the cable meant that in the case of a cable failure, due to breakage or breakdown of insulation, the position of the fault could be calculated from the reading of the galvanometer.

One curious phenomenon observed at the shore end of the cable was due to the fact that the iron hull of the Great Eastern, and the

13 *Great Eastern* at sea

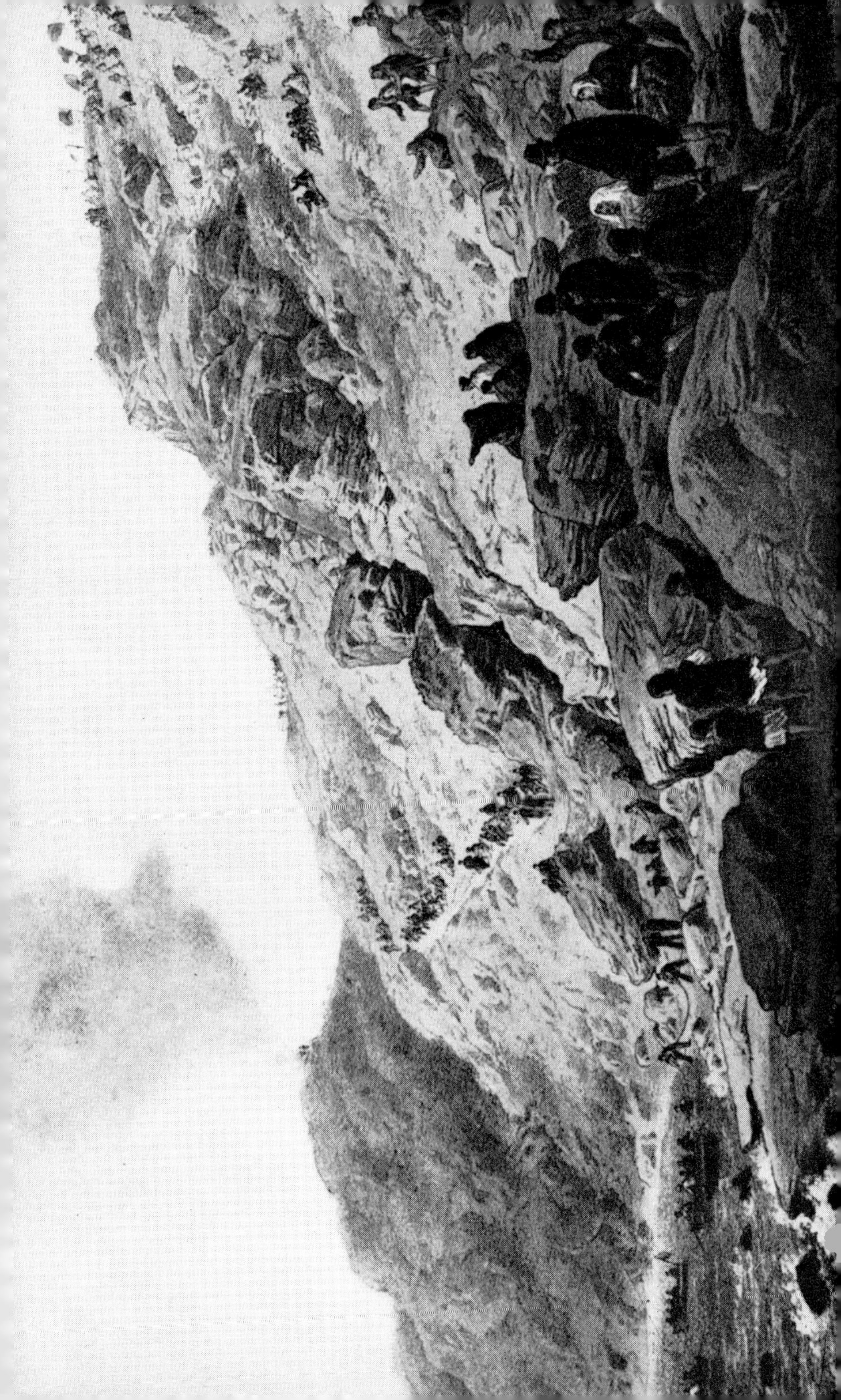

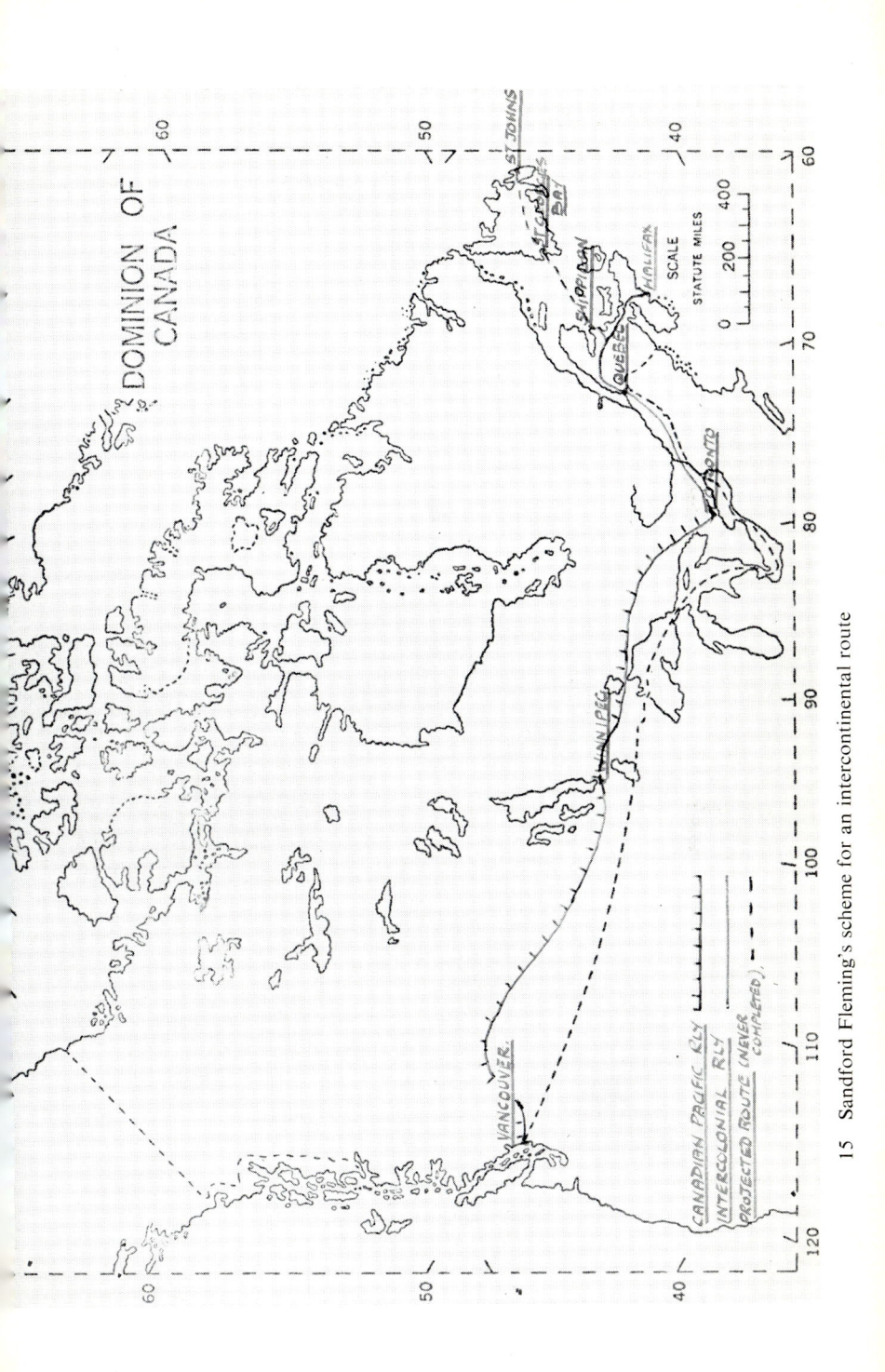

15 Sandford Fleming's scheme for an intercontinental route

16 Locomotive *A. L. Blackman*, Newfoundland Railway, 1882

17 Locomotive *St. John's*, Newfoundland Railway, 1882

18 Locomotive *193*, Reid Newfoundland Railway, 1920

19 Harbour Grace from the Railway, about 1900

20 Derailment of locomotive near King's Bridge Road, St. John's

21 Locomotive *193* preserved at Bowater Park, Cornerbrook, 1967

22 St. John's Railway Station

23   Locomotive *939* (diesel electric), Newfoundland Railway

three huge coils of cable which it contained formed a giant electromagnet. Because of this it was possible for the watchers ashore to detect the rolling of the ship faithfully reproduced by the galvanometer. The iron sheath of the cable also had the effect of upsetting *Great Eastern's* compass. Because of the huge quantity of iron in the ship itself, the standard compass had been placed at the top of one of the masts, being visible from the bridge by means of a periscope arrangement. But with the extra iron of the cable even this was not enough, and so the navigation was left to H.M.S. *Sphinx* which *Great Eastern* followed at a discreet distance.

The machinery for paying out the cable had been designed by Samuel Canning and built by the well-known firm of engineers Messrs. Penn & Co. of Greenwich. It was an improved version of that fitted to *Agamemnon* and *Niagara*, but although very efficient at paying out the cable, it had one great drawback. It could not be reversed to haul in cable should that be necessary. For this purpose a separate engine and winch was fitted in the bows. This was to have serious consequences before long.

On the day after starting, when eighty-four miles out, a fault developed. In the caboose the beam of light leapt off the scale, and the electrician on watch jumped to his feet to beat the gong hanging outside the door. This was the signal to the bridge to heave to and stop cable-laying. It was calculated that the fault lay between ten and sixty miles astern, and so it was decided to pick up back to the fault. Unfortunately this was no easy job. Because the cable could only be hauled in from the bows, it was necessary to cut the cable after a retaining stopper had been put on it, and then manhandle the end down the side of the ship (one-eighth of a mile long) past rigging, lifeboats, and other obstructions, until it could be attached to the winding-in engine at the bows. This was done successfully and the great ship turned and retraced her path, winding in cable as she went.

All night they wound it in, and as it came over the side, coated in the grey ooze of the Atlantic bottom, the engineers examined each foot. At ten and a half miles back they found the fault. A piece of iron wire had pierced the cable diametrically, so as to make contact between the sea and the conductor. The faulty section was cut out, the cable laboriously moved back to the stern, and spliced, and paying out commenced again, while communication was re-established with the operators in Ireland, who had been waiting anxiously by a dead line for twelve hours.

For two days all went smoothly. Through the cable news was received on board that Gooch had been elected, in his absence, Conservative Member of Parliament for Cricklade. He was to sit in the House of Commons through four Parliaments and never make a maiden speech—a performance which, he once remarked, some other members might do well to emulate.

With other news this appeared in *Great Eastern*'s newspaper, *The Atlantic Telegraph*, which was published on board and illustrated by Robert Dudley. Its heading showed a pair of field glasses (a play on the names of Messrs. Field and Glass) flanked by the British and American flags.

In front of *Great Eastern* steamed the escort *Sphinx*, navigating and taking soundings. Around the two of them moved *Terrible*, warning passing ships away from their paths as the cable spun smoothly over the stern of the leviathan down to the bottom nearly three miles below. It was noted in the electricians' caboose that as the depth to which the cable descended increased, so its insulating property increased, probably as a result of the fall in temperature.

By July 29th, 716 miles of cable had been laid, and all seemed to be going well, when another and more serious fault developed. Once again the arduous task of picking up cable commenced. After nine hours' work, the fault was safe inboard and the recovered section was cut out. Once again the splice was made and laying recommenced. The faulty section was examined carefully by de Sauty, and another piece of iron wire was discovered sticking right through the core. This was too much to dismiss as an accident, and inevitably misgivings were now felt by all on board, for it seemed that the two faults could only have been caused by someone attempting to sabotage the cable. Who, and why, remained a mystery.

Strict discipline was enforced. No one was allowed on deck unless he was working, and a watch was set in each of the cable tanks.

By August 2nd they were two-thirds of the way across and 1,186 miles of cable had been laid when, just as dawn was breaking, a third fault was reported. Once again a splinter of iron had pierced the cable, but this time it had been spotted in the cable tank where Cyrus Field himself was on watch. A warning was shouted to the deck cablemen, but before the ship could be stopped the faulty cable had disappeared over the side. At least, however, the sabotage theory had been disposed of. The splinter had been recognised as a piece of the armouring wire which had been broken off in the tank and had worked its way into the cable.

For the third time the process of getting in the cable was begun. The cut was made and the end, secured by a stopper, was carried to the pick-up gear at the bows and winding-in began. Suddenly, without any warning the cable parted, flew through the hawse-pipe and vanished into the sea. So quickly had it happened that nothing could be done to stop it, and the cablemen stood speechless, stunned by this sudden misfortune.

There was only one thing to be done, and Samuel Canning lost no time in carrying it out. He at once decided to attempt to grapple the lost cable 2,000 fathoms (12,000 feet) below. The *Great Eastern* turned and steamed fourteen miles into the wind, while a small five-hook grapnel and five miles of wire rope were got ready. Then the great ship turned, hoisted sail, and for the first and only time in her life moved under canvas alone. She sailed to and fro at right angles across the line of the cable, while the grapnel and its wire were lowered from the bows.

When three miles of wire had been let out the strain shown by the dynamometer decreased. Presumably the grapnel had reached bottom. Slowly and silently the huge ship glided along, trailing the line over the sea-bed. It was, as someone put it 'like fishing with a bent pin and string from the top of St. Paul's'.

All through the night this went on, and then at 6 a.m. on August 3rd the dynamometer measured a strain on the wire. The grapnel had hooked something on the bottom, but it might only be a rock. *Great Eastern* hove to, and started to wind in. The line came up, and the pull remained steady. It must be the cable. For hours they reeled it in till 700 fathoms of wire had been recovered. Once the wire snapped, but the brakeman stopped it before it ran out. At 700 fathoms, however, a shackle between two lengths of wire rope broke, and down went the cable and grapnel.

They marked the spot with a buoy and steamed away to try again. But now the fog came down and the wind dropped, and they must wait for the weather to improve. At last, on the fifth day the fog lifted and the wind was in the right direction. Sails were hoisted and a second grapnel lowered.

Once again they caught something and began to reel in. Slowly the line came up, until a mile of wire had been recovered and then, just as before, a swivel parted and the line disappeared over the side. There was still enough line left, however, and nothing daunted, on the eighth day, after losing the buoy in a gale, Canning again tried to fish for the cable. This time his line was made up of an odd assortment of wire rope, hemp, and manilla. For the third time a grapnel was lowered and trailed along the sea-bed. Again they hooked the elusive cable and commenced to wind in. The suspense on board *Great Eastern* was almost unbearable as hour after hour the cable was slowly wound up. As each shackle jarred over the winch the cable-men held their breath. Those not required on deck stayed below rather than witness it. Suddenly, when the cable was within 1,500 fathoms of the surface, and the strain had reached the figure of 9 tons, yet another shackle parted and the precious load plunged to the bottom of the Atlantic.

The supply of grappling wire was now exhausted and nothing more could be done. *Great Eastern* signalled to her escorts that she was returning home and set course for Valentia. Yet another attempt to lay a cable across the Atlantic had failed.

Great Eastern sailed home leaving £600,000 worth of capital on the floor of the Atlantic ocean. The most disappointed man on board must have been Cyrus Field, but never for a moment did he give up hope.

The last attempt had demonstrated that in *Great Eastern* they had the ideal ship for the enterprise and they had come nearer than ever to a satisfactory attempt. As soon as the company could raise the money they would try again; nor were the directors despondent, and at the first meeting after the return of *Great Eastern* they resolved not only to retrieve the lost cable, but to lay a new one as well.

The contractors were prepared to make a new cable at a cost of £500,000, and would demand no payment until the cable was operating. In that case, they were also to receive £100,000 in shares of the Atlantic Telegraph Company. Moreover, they offered to raise the old cable and complete it, assuming all the necessary risks.

To these terms the Atlantic Telegraph Company agreed, and set out to raise another £600,000. They issued 120,000 £5 preference shares, and such was the interest that had now been aroused in the project that the shares were over-subscribed. Unfortunately, someone found that the company had acted illegally. Their Memorandum of Association made no provision for the issue of preference shares, and so the money had to be handed back to the subscribers. It certainly seemed as if the fates were against the company.

Once again it was Daniel Gooch who came to their rescue in the hour of need, as he had done with the purchase of *Great Eastern*. His training had been as an engineer, and his early days had been spent in the engine sheds of the Great Western Railway in the days when the steam locomotive was a very uncertain machine. When Queen Victoria made her first journey by rail in 1841, Gooch was on the footplate at the controls. It was as a locomotive engineer that he became famous, but in later years he proved himself just as able as a capitalist and man of business. After what he had seen on *Great Eastern*'s first trip he was convinced of the eventual success of the Atlantic telegraph. He now suggested that an entirely new company be formed which could raise the required capital and then be amalgamated with the Atlantic Telegraph Company. He himself offered to subscribe £20,000 to the new company, though in the event this proved unnecessary. Thomas Brassey offered £60,000.

The new company was duly formed and the required capital was soon forthcoming; in fact the money was subscribed even before the prospectus was issued and the books opened to the public. Most of it came from the main contractors, the Telegraph Construction and Maintenance Company and from subcontractors. When the required capital was raised, the concern amalgamated with the Atlantic Telegraph Company, to form a new organisation, the Anglo-American Telegraph Company, the directors of the old Atlantic Telegraph Company retaining control.

Work immediately got under way to prepare for the laying of a new cable in the summer of 1866. It was proposed not only to do this, but also to repair and complete the one lying at the bottom of the sea. Another 1,600 miles of cable was ordered from the makers. This, with what was still on board *Great Eastern*, would be enough for both projects, with 113 miles in reserve.

The new length of cable had some slight modifications: a lighter but stronger armouring which was now galvanised, and improvements to the heavier shore ends. A new system of continuous testing of the insulation was devised.

Work was also carried out on *Great Eastern*. Two feet of barnacles were scraped off her bottom, giving her another knot of speed. Her engines and boilers were overhauled, and twenty miles of grappling wire provided. Most important of all, her paying-out machinery was modified so that it could be used for picking up cable, and a 70 horse-power engine fitted to it for this purpose. In this way the risk involved in changing the cable from the stern to the bows could be avoided. The picking-up machinery in the bows was retained for use in grappling for lost cable, and fitted with a pair of 70 horse-power engines. The two vessels which were to accompany *Great Eastern*—S.S. *Medway* and S.S. *Albany*—were also fitted up with similar gear.

The twenty miles of grappling rope was made of seven strands, each strand consisting of 49 iron wires separately covered with manilla hemp. It could stand a strain of 30 tons. Various kinds of grapnels were put on board; some with spring retainers to the hooks to keep the cable from escaping; others fashioned like pincers, and yet others which could cut the cable before raising it. All this equipment was supplied by the firm of Brown, Lenox & Co. As before, *Great Eastern* loaded her cable at Sheerness and on June 30th, 1866, sailed for Ireland with *Medway* and *Albany*. Arriving at Valentia they were joined by H.M.S. *Terrible* and H.M.S. *Racoon*, who were under orders to accompany the expedition.

This time there were no crowds at Valentia to greet them, and no junketings or celebrations. There had been too many failures by now, and yet another attempt excited no popular interest. On July 7th the collier *William Cory* (commonly known as 'Dirty Billy') landed the shore end of the cable in Foilhummerum Bay and laid out twenty-seven miles to the great ship. On board *Great Eastern*, Daniel Gooch noted in his diary that one of the tugs attending them was named *Brunel* and regarded this as a good omen for the voyage.

On July 13th they took the end of the cable on board from the 'Dirty Billy', spliced to it, and when all was ready weighed anchor and slipped quietly out to sea in a fog. This time there was no cheering, no sense of occasion. It was all part of the day's work. The fact that July 13th was a Friday passed without comment.

On board in charge of the laying once again was Mr. Canning, but de Sauty's place as Chief Electrician was now taken by Mr.

Willoughby Smith. Sir Charles Bright was no longer consultant, having become M.P. for Greenwich, and his place was taken by his partner Mr. Latimer Clarke, who took up his quarters at Valentia. With H.M.S. *Terrible* leading, the convoy steamed at a speed of five knots across a calm sea. It seemed at last as though the fates were kind. Cable laying proceeded smoothly, except for two occasions when fouls occurred in the tanks due to broken sheathing wires catching neighbouring turns. In each case the ship hove to and the fouls were cleared in time. By Thursday, July 19th, the after tank was emptied and on July 24th the forward tank. Only the midships tank remained to be laid. Life proceeded quietly on board; the ship's newspaper was posted up daily with the latest news gleaned from the telegraph; a concert was organised. Constantly the electricians tested the cable and exchanged messages with Valentia.

On July 25th they ran into fog on the Grand Banks. The convoy reduced speed and maintained its position by siren. On the 27th they met H.M.S. *Niger* which had been waiting in Newfoundland for them, and on the same day they entered Trinity Bay, and at the little township of Heart's Content dropped anchor at the end of their voyage, fourteen days after leaving Valentia. Heart's Content is some eighteen miles from Bull Arm, where the 1858 cable had been landed. It was chosen in preference as being more protected and with deeper water.

In England, the directors of the Anglo-American Telegraph Company heard the news in the following message.

'Great Eastern
Heart's Content,
27th July, 1866.

'We arrived here at 9 o'clock this morning. Thank God, the cable is laid, and is in perfect working order.

CYRUS FIELD'

For the last three nights of the voyage Field had been unable to sleep as the successful end of his scheme drew nearer. For twelve years he had worked for this moment—twelve years of set-backs and heart-breaks that would have daunted most men, and now at last it was accomplished. In his moment of triumph he issued the following statement to the press:

'I cannot find words suitable to convey my admiration for the men who have so ably conducted the nautical, engineering and electrical departments of this enterprise amid difficulties which must be seen to be appreciated. In fact, all on board the telegraph fleet, and all connected with the enterprise have done their best to have the cable made and laid in perfect condition, and He who rules the wind and waves has crowned their united efforts with perfect success.'

Later in the day the end of the cable was brought ashore and taken to the building which housed the overland telegraph. In the Newfoundland Museum at St. John's there is a painting of this scene. A sea mist (or fog, as Newfoundlanders would call it) hangs over the bay. In the distance can be dimly seen the strange outline of *Great Eastern*, while a string of boats supports the cable ashore, watched by a crowd of villagers with a sprinkling of red-coated soldiers. In the foreground sailors bear the end of the cable on to dry land, like some strange captured sea monster. The excitement as it reached shore was tremendous; Gooch records that the sailors capered about as they stepped ashore and one even put the end of the cable in his mouth and sucked it. In St. John's all the church bells were set ringing, and at Heart's Content a small harmonium was brought down to the shore and a Te Deum sung with prayers of thanksgiving for the successful accomplishment of the venture. As soon as the cable end reached the relay station the electricians set to work fixing up the instruments; six operators came ashore from *Great Eastern* and in a very short time messages were being relayed to the American continent. It was something of an anticlimax for Field, however, when he discovered that messages could not be relayed direct, as the New York, Newfoundland, and London Company had neglected to keep their link in order and the cable across the straits from Newfoundland to Cape Breton was not working, messages having to be passed by steamer. Thus it was that while a message from Queen Victoria arrived on the same day that the cable was landed, the reply from the President of the United States did not get to Heart's Content until four days later. The messages were as follows:

'From H.M. The Queen, Osborne.
'To the President of the United States, Washington.
    'The Queen congratulates the President on the successful comple-

tion of the undertaking which she hopes may serve as an additional bond of union between the United States and England.'

(Received on board *Great Eastern* 27th July, 1866; commenced receiving 11.28 a.m.; finished receiving 11.49 a.m.)

'From the President of the United States, Executive Mansion, Washington.
'To H.M. the Queen of the United Kingdom of Britain and Ireland.
'The President of the United States acknowledges with profound gratification the receipt of Her Majesty's message and cordially reciprocates the hope that the cable which now unites the Eastern and Western hemispheres may serve to strengthen and perpetuate peace and amity between the governments of England and the Republic of the United States of America.
'Andrew Johnson.'

(Received at Heart's Content Station from New York July 31st at 3.42 p.m.

Commenced sending 3.50 p.m.; finished sending 4.01 p.m.; received in London 4.11 p.m.; delivered to the Queen 5.00 p.m.)

Field also received, on the same day, a personal message from the President of the United States. It read as follows:

'From the President of the United States
'To Cyrus Field, Esq., Heart's Content, Newfoundland.
'I heartily congratulate you and trust that your enterprise may prove as successful as your efforts have been persevering. May the cable under the sea tend to promote and to perpetuate peace between the Republic of the West and the Governments of the Eastern Hemisphere.
'Sg. Andrew Johnson.'

The technical improvements in the submarine cable had been matched by advances in the design of the receiving instruments. For the 1866 cable Professor Thompson had produced an improvement on the mirror galvanometer: the siphon recorder. In this instrument the moving coil of the galvanometer had no mirror, but was attached by two silk threads to a lightly poised fine glass tube which formed a siphon. The top end rested in an ink-well, and the lower end on a moving strip of paper, which unrolled from one reel to another, driven by clockwork. The glass tube thus drew a continuous ink-line on the paper. When a signal was received by the galvanometer, the movement of the coil operating through the silk cords pulled the glass tube to one side or the other, thus producing deflections in the ink line which represented 'dots' or 'dashes'. The siphon recorder had two great advantages over the old type of instrument. Firstly, messages could be sent much more quickly, as the speed was no longer governed by the capacity of the mirror clerk to read light signals. This meant more traffic over the line with the attendant commercial advantages. Secondly, there was a permanent record of each message, should there be any need to refer to it. The siphon recorder became the standard instrument for submarine cables throughout the world for many years.

Commercial use of the telegraph began almost immediately, and after the first day Daniel Gooch was able to record in his diary with satisfaction: 'Yesterday we had 50 messages, paying us, I suppose, not less than £1200.'

The price charged at first was £20 for twenty words, and £1 for each aditional word, but as the speed of transmission increased, this rate was progressively lowered. By the end of the century it had fallen to one shilling a word. This time the cable was treated with proper respect, and continued to give good service until 1872, by which time other cables had been laid.

CHAPTER 4

Success

THE 'GREAT EASTERN'S' work was not yet done. At Heart's Content she took on board 600 miles of extra cable from S.S. *Medway* and then re-coaled. Six colliers had been sent out in advance from Cardiff with 8,000 tons of fuel. One had been lost at sea, and the others had been waiting at St. John's. They now moved down to Heart's Content to replenish the great ship's bunkers. This done, she left to search for the lost cable of 1865 and to attempt to raise it.

H.M S. *Terrible* and S.S. *Albany* had left a week before to start the search. It was not an easy task, as all the marker buoys had long since been swept away. However, when *Great Eastern* joined them at the rendezvous, 600 miles from Newfoundland, *Albany* had already hooked the cable at a depth of two and a half miles, but had lost it before it could be hauled in. The *Great Eastern* made her first drag on August 13th, about fifteen miles from the end of the cable. They lifted it 1,300 fathoms before the line broke.

Throughout August the dragging continued and no less than thirty attempts were made. On one tantalising occasion the cable had actually been raised to the surface, and while it was being made fast the grapnel canted, the line slipped off its prongs like a great eel, and disappeared into the sea. By the end of August the store of grappling wire was nearly exhausted and the weather was worsening, so a change of tactics was decided upon. The ships moved eighty miles to the eastward, where the depth was not so great. The cable was grappled and raised to about 900 fathoms from the surface and there suspended from a buoy. *Great Eastern* then moved three miles west and grappled the cable again. Farther west still *Medway* grappled the cable and cut it. *Great Eastern* now had a bight of cable which was free at one end and suspended from a buoy at the other. This she was able to raise without difficulty, and a little before 1 a.m. on September 2nd the long-lost cable made its appearance amid breathless silence. The end was secured, hoisted aboard, and taken to the caboose under the bridge for testing.

At Valentia the cable, which had been dead for over a year, was connected up to a mirror galvanometer and a watch kept from the time *Great Eastern* left Heart's Content on August 9th. Twenty-three days passed and the staff at the little wooden telegraph station had almost given up hope, when at 5.45 a.m. on Sunday, September 2nd, the clerk on watch, a Mr. Crocker, saw a sudden flicker from the spot of light. A few seconds of unsteady jumping followed, and then the telegraph began to speak. 'Ship to shore; I have much pleasure in speaking to you through the 1865 cable. Just going to make splice.'

It was a dramatic moment which put a seal on the success of the whole expedition. For Cyrus Field, on board the *Great Eastern*, it was the culmination of all his efforts and he records that he was so moved that he had to retire to his cabin. For the first time he could not restrain his tears.

The recovered end was spliced on at once, and by seven o'clock the great ship was steaming back to Heart's Content laying cable as she went. By the evening of September 8th the end of the cable had been landed and two lines of communication now existed across the Atlantic. Cyrus Field's great project had been completed.

Its completion was accompanied by the jubilations that usually marked such occasions in those days. The honour of knighthood was conferred on Samuel Canning, Captain Anderson, Professor Thompson, Daniel Gooch and others connected with the enterprise. As soon as *Great Eastern* arrived in the Mersey a banquet was given by the Liverpool Chamber of Commerce in honour of the successful completion, the first of many such occasions in Britain and America.

The speeches that marked these celebrations followed the usual pattern of eulogy that these occasions demand, but at least one of them is worthy of mention. In a speech at a dinner given in his honour at New York, Cyrus Field had this to say.

'Of the results of this enterprise—commercially and politically— it is for others to speak. To one effect only do I refer as the wish of my heart—that is, as it brings us into closer relationship with England it may produce a better understanding between the two countries. Let who will speak against England—words of censure must come from other lips than mine. I have received too much kindness of Englishmen to join in this language. I have eaten of their bread and drunk of their cup, and I have received of them in the darkest hours of this enterprise words of cheer which I can never forget; and if any words of mine can tend to peace and goodwill they shall not be wanting. I close with the sentence—England and America clasping hands across the sea—may this firm grasp be a pledge of friendship to all generations.'

Frederic Gisborne's telegraph link across Newfoundland, which had been the beginning of the great enterprise, did not survive long after the completion of the Atlantic Telegraph. It was already outdated and unreliable. The submarine cable across the straits to Cape Breton was constantly out of order (always, it seemed, at a crucial moment), and this is hardly surprising. In the Newfoundland Museum at St. John's there is a short length of this cable which was brought up by fishermen 'jigging' for cod near Cape Ray in 1919. It is composed of a seven-strand copper core, covered with gutta-percha to a diameter of $\frac{3}{8}$ inch. It has no outer covering. To compare it with a piece of the 1866 cable in the same display is to realise how far the science of submarine cable laying had progressed in those twelve years.

The upkeep of the overland line from Heart's Content to Cape Ray was also a constant worry. For most of its length it crossed wild and desolate country where in winter snow could bring down wires and poles and render maintenance work hazardous and full of hardship. Where it passed through inhabited country there were hazards of a different sort. Acts passed by the Newfoundland Legislature at this time, providing penalties for the damage of telegraph lines, suggest that some of the local inhabitants were not above removing portions of wire for their own use. There were also the boys 'firing rocks' at the insulators (there still are today). So in 1867, a year after the transatlantic cable was laid, the Anglo-American Telegraph Company decided to lay a submarine cable from Heart's Content around the coast of Newfoundland to Cape Breton. This took the place of the overland line, which fell into disuse. Heart's Content then became a relay station for the cable, though it was, of course, still linked by land line with the rest of Newfoundland for local purposes.

The southern part of Newfoundland is still as wild and uninhabited today as when the telegraph was laid across it over a hundred years ago. Does any trace now remain of that line with its four-foot wide path and bridges over the waterways, built at great cost and only used fully for a year? Probably not, but it is intriguing to surmise.

As for *Great Eastern*, the laying of the Atlantic cable was the opening of a new phase in her life, which was to prove more successful than anything that had gone before. In the next seven years, under a new commander, Captain Robert Halpin, she laid 26,000 miles of cable including the direct cable to India in 1869, the 'all red' line. For the first and only time in her life she traced the route for which her designer had intended her, and, painted white, entered the harbour of Bombay. To do so she had to go round the Cape. The Suez Canal was not big enough for the Great Ship. From Bombay she laid the cable to Aden, then retraced her wake back to the Atlantic. In the ensuing years Gooch and his partners chartered her to many different companies; they were the only owners successfully to employ the great leviathan. Her career came to an end in 1874 when the first custom-built cable ship came into commission. This was a vessel of 4,935 tons, and the second largest ship afloat. It was planned to name her *Great Western*, but in the event she received the more prosaic title of *T. S. Hooper*. It was fitting that the last task of *Great Eastern* should be the laying of a new Atlantic cable for the Anglo-American Co. in 1874 (she had already laid one replacement in 1873). The wheel had come full circle for the great ship. This time she spun her web from Valentia to Heart's Content without incident and without any attention from the outside world. Cable laying had become a matter of routine. On her last voyage back from Newfoundland she forged another and more personal link between that country and England. Captain Halpin had married a Newfoundland girl, a Miss Munn, daughter of a St. John's merchant, and their honeymoon was the last voyage of *Great Eastern*. From Heart's Content she proceeded home to Milford Haven, there to be laid up for the next eleven years. Her great paddle wheels never turned again, and her screw only for a few brief hours, to propel her to Liverpool where she finished her days ignominiously as an advertisement hoarding and floating fun-fair, under charter to a Liverpool department store.

Of the cables she had laid across the Atlantic, the first one, that of 1865, remained in use until 1877. The second one, laid in 1866, had a shorter life, succumbing in 1872. Her third and fourth, the 1873 and 1874 cables, are still in use today, though the greater parts of them have been renewed.

Cyrus Field, the chief projector of the scheme, received a vote of thanks from the United States Congress, and also a gold medal, as well as numerous recognitions from all over the world. Few honours have been more richly deserved. With the completion of the Atlantic cable, however, he turned his interest in other directions. He had no interest in submarine cables as such. The project of a transatlantic cable he had accepted as a challenge and with its completion he turned his energies in other directions. He promoted railways and newspapers and was President of the New York Elevated Railway Company until his death in 1892.

PART TWO
THE GREAT AMERICAN AND EUROPEAN SHORT LINE RAILWAY

CHAPTER 5

Sandford Fleming and His Vision

WITH THE COMPLETION of the Atlantic cable, Newfoundland became an outpost of the North American continent, the last link on the line of telegraphic communication to Europe. It was inevitable that before long someone would consider the possibility of using this island, with its unique position, for some other form of communication beside the telegraph. Why not use it as an outpost for the North American railway system, a terminus from which fast ships could carry passengers to Europe, thus saving days of uncomfortable sea travel? The idea followed quickly after the establishment of the first telegraph cable in 1858, and credit for putting it into the form of a practical proposal must go to one of the great pioneers of railway building, Sandford Fleming.

Sir Sandford Fleming, as he later became, was a great civil engineer. He was more than that, however; he was a man of rare vision. Behind all his schemes there was a sense of purpose far beyond that of most of his contemporaries. From early on in his career he dreamed of a transcontinental railway from the Pacific to the Atlantic. In the days when Canada was still a collection of separate provinces he saw the value of such a line as the medium which would enable the separate provinces to come together in a dominion; but more than that he visualised a railway stretching out to the easternmost point of the North American continent to connect to Europe by the shortest sea route. Over such a line, he thought, would come traffic from Europe for all parts of the United States and Canada, for the Pacific coast, and even for such distant places as Australia, New Zealand, and Japan. And where else would be the Atlantic terminus of such a railway except in Newfoundland, at St. John's?

In due course Sandford Fleming saw the first part of his dream come true, for he was the creator of the Intercolonial Railway, which linked the Maritime Provinces, on the Atlantic coast, with Ontario, and the even greater project of the Canadian Pacific Railway which carried the line westward to the Pacific. If the rest of his grand scheme had succeeded, the line would have extended farther to the east, across Newfoundland, and St. John's would have become a great ocean terminus, with fast liners arriving daily from Liverpool. Through it would have passed most of the traffic to North America. It is interesting to speculate on the effect this might have had on the development of Newfoundland. For half a century the country would have enjoyed the prosperity such a traffic would have brought, only to lose it when the development of the Atlantic greyhounds made the passage to New York a matter of four to five days. Perhaps it was as well that Sandford Fleming's scheme never came to fruition as far as Newfoundland was concerned. That it did not do so was in no way due to lack of effort on his part, but rather to political difficulties which he could not overcome.

Like many engineers of his time, Sandford Fleming was a Scot. He was born at Kirkcaldy in Fife, and was educated at Kirkcaldy Burgh School, where Thomas Carlyle also received his education. At 14 he left to become the pupil of a well-known engineer and surveyor, John Lang. In 1841 there was plenty of scope for a budding engineer to obtain experience, with the rapid growth of railways and public works. Fleming's training was obtained on surveys for harbours and waterworks as well as railway surveys on the lines from Edinburgh to Perth, and Perth to Dundee through the Carse of Gowrie.

In January 1845 he became qualified to practise as a civil engineer and draughtsman. Prospects were bright in Britain with the continuing growth of the railway system, but like many another youngster the spirit of adventure had got hold of him, and after careful thought he decided to try his future in the new world. Accordingly, at the age of 18 he sailed with his two brothers from Glasgow aboard a timber ship bound for Canada. For £4 10s. each they shipped on the sailing ship *Brilliant* and put out from the Broomielaw on April 24th. They arrived at Quebec on June 5th, so that on the voyage Fleming had plenty of time to reflect on the opportunities for speeding up travel on the North Atlantic.

The three brothers landed in a country very different from the Canada of today. It consisted then of two parts; Upper Canada and Lower Canada, or what are now the Provinces of Ontario and Quebec. It was still a pioneering country; its cities were only settlements, and there should have been no lack of work for a trained civil engineer. Yet Fleming had great difficulty in finding employment; so much so that at one time he thought of taking to farming. In his travels, however, he landed up at Toronto, and having nothing else to do, set about making a survey of the town with the idea of selling the resulting maps. He completed his survey but could find no lithographer to print his work, so he set out to teach himself the art. He had to find his own stones and prepare them, engrave them, and finally print from them. The maps which he produced not only provided him with a livelihood, but led to a government surveying contract which set him on the road to success. His success at the art of engraving can be judged from the fact that in 1851 he was given the task of producing the design of Canada's first postage stamp. If genius is an infinite capacity for taking pains, then Sandford Fleming unquestionably possessed that kind of genius.

But Fleming's great interest was civil engineering and in particular the pioneering of new enterprises. In 1852 he got his chance, and a job after his own heart, with his appointment to the post of Assistant Engineer for the construction of the Ontario, Simcoe, and Huron Railroad. This line (later known by the simpler title of the Northern Railroad) ran for some seventy miles from Toronto north-west to Collingwood, at the foot of Lake Huron. There were two Assistant Engineers on this project, and Fleming's colleague was a man with a name famous in the world of railway engineering. He was Alfred Brunel, but although a railway engineer, he was no relation of the great I.K., builder of the Great Western Railway and designer of *Great Eastern*.

The Northern Railroad was one of the early railways in Canada and typical of the pioneer lines in that country. Because their object was to open up virgin country and connect scattered communities, they differed greatly from railways in Britain, which connected heavily populated towns relatively short distances apart, thus requiring a high density of traffic moving at maximum speeds. In Canada this high-density, high-speed traffic was not required, and so it was possible to build railways of a different standard. They were invariably single-track lines, with a permanent way that was much less substantial than that used in Britain. There was abundance of wood, but iron had to be brought considerable distances and was expensive, so the early railways were often laid with wooden rails, on the tops of which strips of iron were fastened. The passing of a train would often loosen a strip so that the end of it would spring upward, with disastrous results for the next train that came. Because of this they were known as 'snake rails'.

Sandford Fleming did not have to lay the Northern Railroad with snake rails, but nevertheless the rails he used were only 35 lb. per yard—a weight which was often exceeded on narrow-gauge lines in Britain. There was no shortage of timber for sleepers, or ties, however, so they could be spaced closely together. Also, high speeds were not required, and locomotives with bar frames and leading bogie trucks together with bogie rolling stock did not require such a solid road. The engines of the Northern Railroad were of this kind; 'American' type 4-4-0 locomotives with wagon-top boilers, big spark arresters on the chimneys, and a spherical sand-box mounted centrally on the boiler. They were very definitely products of the special conditions for which they were required.

For three years Sandford Fleming worked on the Northern Railroad as Assistant Engineer, during which time he surveyed much of the line. Then in 1855 he became Chief Engineer, a post he held until 1863. During this time his idea of a transcontinental railway was born. He saw the tiny Northern Railroad as a link in a great railway spanning North America from ocean to ocean. In 1862 he published a treatise entitled *Practical Observations on the Construction of a Continuous Line of Railway from Canada to the Pacific Ocean on British Territory*.

The appearance of this work led to an approach to Fleming from a committee representing the people living in the Red River area. The Red River, which rises in Minnesota and flows northward over the border and into Lake Winnipeg, is in the centre of British North America. In Fleming's time it ran through an isolated settlement in the middle of the prairies, at the spot which is the city of Winnipeg today.

The people of the Red River Settlement wanted a road built from Lake Superior to the Red River as part of a larger project—they regarded it as a preliminary step towards a line of railway that would eventually traverse British North America from ocean to ocean. This transcontinental railway scheme was one that had already engaged the minds of several far-sighted men; men of big ideas; men like Sandford Fleming who possessed that rare combination of common sense and imagination which provides the driving force behind all great enterprises. The average man could find in such a project, at such a time, nothing short of madness. He saw only a number of scattered and straggling colonies, east and west, with an immense wilderness, practically uninhabited, between them. The idea of building a road or even a railway through such a country did not seem worthy of serious consideration. On the other hand the man of ideas looked into the future, saw these isolated communities linked together with a line of steel, and the uninhabited wilderness part of a dominion peopled from sea to sea. Because Fleming was just such a man the people of the Red River settlement chose him to present their case, and because he believed whole-heartedly in their proposals, and because of his firm faith in the destiny of his adopted country, Fleming agreed to their request and threw himself enthusiastically into the project.

First he met the representatives of the Red River settlers and helped them to draft a memorial, setting out their case. Their idea of a road, to be followed later by a railway fitted in exactly with Fleming's own ideas. In his treatise he had put forward the principle that in developing communications in new countries the order of priority should be first the telegraph, then roads, and finally railways.

When their proposals had been put in the form of a memorial he took it to Sir John Macdonald, Prime Minister of Canada, which still consisted of only the two provinces, Upper and Lower Canada. With Sir John's approval he set out for London to put his proposals before the Imperial Government.

At the Colonial Office he found little enthusiasm for his ideas. He was passed from one department to another and from official to official, experiencing all the frustrations of a projector of visionary schemes up against the caution of civil servants. Fleming, however, was not the man to be put off by red tape, and at length he was successful in obtaining an interview with the Colonial Secretary, the Duke of Newcastle.

Somewhat to his surprise, for he was now prepared for any rebuff, he found himself in the presence of a quiet unassuming gentleman who welcomed him cordially and listened with sympathetic attention to the plea of the Red River settlers for transportation. The Duke had accompanied the Prince of Wales on his tour of Canada three years before, and knew something of the country. He gave

Sandford Fleming a careful hearing, but could hold out no hope of financial help from the Imperial Government. He felt that it was a matter rather for the Government of Canada. So far as its immediate object was concerned, Fleming's mission to England bore no direct fruit, but indirectly, as we shall soon see, it had results of far-reaching importance.

He travelled home on *Great Eastern*, which had not then begun its cable-laying career and was still a passenger ship. No doubt the engineer in Fleming and his curiosity to see the great ship decided his choice. At all events he had a very different passage from his previous one to Canada, taking eight days instead of forty-two. His diary gives a glimpse of life aboard the forerunner of the Atlantic greyhounds. They were at sea for July 4th and the American passengers on board decided that they must celebrate Independence Day in a suitable way. A march around the ship's deck was arranged, and Sandford Fleming was asked by an American friend whether, as a Canadian, he would make a gesture of international friendship by carrying the American flag at the head of the procession. Fleming agreed, on condition that his friend carried the British flag, and this was settled. On the morning of Independence Day the procession formed up on deck ready to proceed. At its head was the Chief Steward's brass band and behind it Sandford Fleming carrying a minute Stars & Stripes, while his American friend was enveloped in an enormous Union Jack. Fleming had arranged with one of the ship's officers to supply him with the largest British and smallest American flags on board. His friend, he records, 'took it like a sport'.

On arriving home at Toronto he found an urgent summons from the Prime Minister, Sir John Macdonald. He hurried to Quebec and was there informed by Sir John that in accordance with arrangements which had been completed with the Imperial Government, a preliminary survey was to be started for the proposed Intercolonial Railway, to run from Quebec through the maritime colonies of New Brunswick and Nova Scotia to some port (possibly Halifax) on the Atlantic seaboard. Such a railway had been suggested many years before, and surveys had actually been carried out but political difficulties prevented any building from taking place. The proposed line ran through territory which was claimed by the United States and which later became the State of Maine. This state projects northwards into Canada, and comes between New Brunswick and Quebec;

and so in order to remain on Canadian soil the Intercolonial Railway would have to make a detour to the north.

Agreement had been reached between the Government of Canada, the administrations of New Brunswick and Nova Scotia, and the Imperial Government in London, which was prepared to guarantee the interest on a loan of £3,000,000 required to build the railway. Under this agreement the survey was to be conducted by a commission of three engineers; one appointed by the Canadian Government, one appointed jointly by the colonies of New Brunswick and Nova Scotia, and the third by the Imperial Government. Sir John Macdonald's purpose in sending for Sandford Fleming was to ask him if he would accept a place on the commission as nominee of the Canadian Government.

There was no question in Fleming's mind about accepting the offer. To him the proposed Intercolonial Railway was simply the first step in his dream of a line from coast to coast, the eastern end of his great Atlantic–Pacific link. The only doubt in his mind was whether the other two members-to-be of the commission would view it in the same light. His doubt was soon resolved, however, for shortly after his visit to Sir John he received a letter from Dr. Charles Tupper representing the colonies of New Brunswick and Nova Scotia. Would Sandford Fleming be their nominee also? There only remained the Imperial Government's nomination, and in October 1863 a letter arrived from the Colonial Office in which the Duke of Newcastle expressed his opinion that Mr. Sandford Fleming, an engineer of 'unexceptionable qualifications' was the man for the job. The visit to London on behalf of the Red River colonists had borne fruit at last, though not in the manner expected. The three-man commission had reduced itself to Sandford Fleming.

He lost no time in getting his survey parties organised and under way. Work had to be done through the winter, and Fleming himself covered much of the ground, moving with his party through uninhabited country snowbound for most of the winter. They went on snowshoes, their instruments and stores carried on dog sleds pulled by three huskies, Gaspé, Wallace, and Bruce. Fortunately for them the area abounded in game, fish, and moose, for Fleming mentions in his diary that the tins of meat supplied to them by a thrifty government quartermaster were found to be left-overs from the Crimean War, and fit only for dumping.

The surveys went on through 1864, and the following year he presented his report to the Canadian Government. In it he reported on no less than fifteen different routes, but the one which he recommended lay to the north skirting the Bay of Chaleur in the Gulf of St. Lawrence and having a branch to the port of Shippigan.

The reasons for this is clear when one studies the report. Fleming had been asked to survey an intercolonial railway—one that would link up the two provinces which constituted Canada with the colonies of New Brunswick and Nova Scotia—and nothing more. But as we have already seen, to him it was something much more. It was the beginning of a potential link between the British Colonies of North America and the continent of Europe. For this purpose he considered Shippigan to be the ideal terminus on the mainland, rather than Halifax. And so, having carried out his terms of reference, he added an appendix to his report, as follows:

'*Remarks on the shortest lines of communication between America and Europe, in connection with the contemplated Intercolonial Railway.*

'In the Northern United States many leading men who take a prominent part in directing the great works of intercommunication of the country have long aimed at an extension of their Railway System to some extreme eastern Port on the Continent: their object being to shorten the Ocean passage and the time of transit between the great commercial centres of the Old and New Worlds.

'A plan was propounded in 1850 by which it was proposed to connect the cities of New York & Boston with Halifax by a railway stretching across the State of Maine and the Provinces of New Brunswick and Nova Scotia.

'The originators and promoters of this plan correctly assumed that the necessities of trade would sooner or later require the adoption of the shortest possible sea voyage between the two Continents.

'It is a question, however, if Halifax would permanently remain the Entrepôt for Ocean Steamers. The same considerations which so strongly influenced the originators of "The European and North American Railway" and which still so powerfully weigh with its promoters, would induce them or their successors to look for a point of embarkation still nearer Europe than Halifax. . . .

'These considerations very naturally lead to reflections on the whole subject of Transatlantic communications and the important question presents itself: what route may ultimately be found the *very speediest* between the Old World and the New?

'Newfoundland, a large Island off the Main Land of North America, and Ireland, an Island off the European Coast, resemble each other in being similar outlying portions of the Continents to which they respectively belong. Possibly they may have a more important similarity and relationship through the remarkable geographical position which they hold, the one to the other, and to the great centres of population and commerce in Europe and America.

'A glance at the Chart of the Atlantic will shew that between Ireland and Newfoundland the Ocean can be spanned by the shortest line.

'Ireland is separated from England and Scotland by the Irish Channel; Newfoundland is separated from this continent by the Gulf of St. Lawrence. Already railways have reached the western coast of Ireland and brought it within sixteen hours of the British capital. Were it possible to introduce the Locomotive into Newfoundland, and establish steam communication between it and the cities of America, a route would be created from Continent to Continent having the Ocean passage reduced to a minimum.

'This route would not be open for traffic throughout the whole year; during certain months the direct course of steamers would be so impeded by floating ice that it could not with certainty or safety be traversed. It therefore remains to be seen whether the route has sufficient advantages while open to recommend its establishment and use during probably not more than seven months of the year.

'In this respect the Newfoundland route must be viewed precisely in the same light as many other lines of traffic on this Continent, and possibly it may be found of equal importance. Of these works may be mentioned the canals of Canada and the United States which, although closed to traffic in winter, have justified the expenditure of enormous sums of money on their original construction, and in repeated enlargements and extensions. Having alluded to the great objection to a route across Newfoundland, we may now proceed to enquire into its merits.

'The track of steamers from the British Coast to New York, and to all points north of New York, passes Ireland and Newfoundland either to the north or to the south; the most usual course however is to the south of both islands. Vessels bound westerly make for

Cape Race on the south-easterly coast of Newfoundland; while those bound easterly make for Cape Clear on the south-westerly angle of Ireland. Not far from Cape Race is the harbour of St. John's and near Cape Clear is the harbour of Valentia; the one the most easterly Port of America, the other is the most westerly Port of Europe. They are distant from each other about 1640 miles. The Irish railways are not yet extended to Valentia, but they have reached Killarney, within about thirty miles of it.

'From St. John's across Newfoundland to the Gulf of St. Lawrence the distance is about 250 miles. On the St. Lawrence coast of the island the Chart shows two harbours, either of which may be found suitable as points of transhipment; the one, St. George's Bay; the other Port-au-Port. They are situated near each other, and both are equally in a direct line from St. John's westerly to the main land. On the westerly shore of the Gulf we find at the entrance to the Bay des Chaleurs the Harbour of Shippigan mentioned in the body of the report on the surveys of the Intercolonial Railway. From St. George's Bay to Shippigan the distance is from 240 to 250 miles. Shippigan may be connected by means of the contemplated Intercolonial Railway with Canada and the United States.

'Although very little is known of the physical features of Newfoundland, from that little we are justified in assuming that the construction of a railway across it from east to west is not impracticable. Perhaps the only white man who has travelled entirely through the interior in the general direction of the projected railway route is Mr. W. E. Cormack. This gentleman travelled across the country many years ago, from Trinity Bay on the east to St. George's Bay on the west. He left the eastern coast about the beginning of September and reached St. George's Harbour on the 2nd of November.

'From Mr. Cormack's account of his journey, it would appear that although a belt along the coast is hilly and broken, much of the interior is comparatively level, consisting of a series of vast savannas. It is more than probable that the interior may be reached by some of the rivers or numerous inlets, which on the map seem to pierce the mountainous belt extending along the margin of the island.

'The line of steam communication from Great Britain across Ireland and Newfoundland and by the contemplated Intercolonial Railway to the interior of North America possesses some important

SANDFORD FLEMING AND HIS VISION

recommendations as will presently be seen. It will however first be necessary to allude to the question of speed.

'At the present time Ocean Steamers generally carry both freight and passengers, and in this respect they are like "mixed trains" on Railways. These mixed trains are employed to serve localities where there is not sufficient passenger and freight traffic to justify the running of special trains. On Railways doing a large business the traffic is properly classified; fast trains are run to carry passengers and mails only, while slow trains are used to convey heavy freight. A similar classification of Ocean traffic may be suggested. Freight will naturally go by the cheapest mode of conveyance, while Passengers and Mails will naturally seek the speediest.

'It is well-known that the shape of a Steamship, other things being equal, governs her speed. The shape again depends on the load, she may be constructed to carry; if the ship is required only for mails and passengers and such voyages as need but a small quantity of fuel, she may be constructed on a model both sharp and light and thus be capable of running more rapidly than if built to carry heavy and bulky loads. A steamship for heavy loads may be compared to a drayhorse, while one made specially for passengers and rapid transit may resemble a race horse, and like the latter the less weight carried the more speed will be made.

'If these views are correct it is clear that the speed of Ocean Steamships might be considerably increased when constructed for a special purpose. The distance between St. John's (Newfoundland) and Valentia is not much more than half the distance between Liverpool and New York; and hence about half the quantity of Coal and Supplies would be required for the Passage between the former points.

'It is quite obvious therefore that a Steamship constructed specially to run between St. John's and Valentia, and for the purpose of carrying only Passengers and Mails, with such light express matter as usually goes by passenger trains, would attain a much higher rate of speed than existing Ocean Steamers. A rate of $16\frac{1}{2}$ miles an hour is thought to be quite possible; the distance between Valentia and St. John's is 1640 miles. At this assumed rate therefore the Ocean passage might be accomplished in 100 hours.

'With regard to the speed on land, it appears from Bradshaw's Railway Guide that the Irish Mails are regularly carried between London and Holyhead at the rate of 40 miles an hour including stoppages, that the Irish Channel is crossed at the rate of 16 miles an hour including the time required for transhipment at Holyhead and Kingstown, and on the completion of a railway to Valentia there is nothing to prevent it being reached from London in the same time now occupied in carrying the mails to Queenstown. . . .

'Although 40 miles an hour is a common rate of speed on the Railways of England it is not usual to run so rapidly on this side of the Atlantic. On the leading passenger routes in the United States, 30 miles an hour including stoppages is attained, although a rate of 25 miles an hour is more commonly adopted. On lines frequently obstructed by snowdrifts, it is not easy to maintain in Winter a rapid rate of transit, but in the Summer with the rail track and rolling stock in a fair condition of repair, there is no difficulty in running at a rate of 30 miles an hour with passenger trains: and therefore this rate of speed may reasonably be assumed as that at which the mails might be carried overland to various points hereafter referred to on this Continent. Having fixed upon a practicable rate of speed by land and water, the time necessary for the conveyance of Mails from London to New York by the projected route may now be ascertained:

'From London to Valentia at present rate of speed in England   16 hours
,, Valentia to St. John's, 1640 miles at 16½ miles an hour   100 hours
,, St. John's to St. George's, 250 miles at 30 miles an hour   8½ hours
,, St. George's to Shippigan, 250 miles at 16½ miles an hour   15½ hours
,, Shippigan to New York, 906 miles at 30 miles an hour   31 hours

Total 171 hours

'It is thus apparent that, without assuming a rate of speed at all extraordinary, it would be possible to carry the Mails from London to New York in 171 hours by the route passing over Ireland, Newfoundland and by the proposed Intercolonial Railway from Shippigan.'

Fleming's report then went on to examine the average times taken by the fastest steamers of the four principal lines operating between New York and Liverpool—the Cunard, Inman, Hamburg and Bremen lines. These varied between 11 days and 13 days 9 hours, against the 7 days 12 hours by Fleming's proposed route. But speed was not the only advantage of his proposals, as he pointed out in these words:

'With regard to the comparative safety of the route, it would seem as if the advantages were greatly in its favour. The portion of the voyage between New York and Liverpool which seamen least fear is that from Ireland to Newfoundland. It is well known that the most dangerous part of the whole voyage is along the American coast between New York and Cape Race, where thick fogs so frequently prevail; this coast line is about 1,000 miles in length and it has been the scene of the larger number of the disasters which have occurred. No less than fourteen or fifteen Ocean steamships have been lost on this portion of the Atlantic Seaboard.

'The route which favours increased security from sea-risks, and which is the shortest in point of time must eventually become the cheapest and in consequence the most frequented. If then the route proposed across Newfoundland and Ireland avoids many of the dangers of existing routes and reduces the Ocean passage proper to 100 hours would not the current of travel naturally seek this route in preference to others, especially when time would be saved thereby?'

With regard to the passenger potential of his proposed route, Fleming had this to say:

'The number and tonnage of Steamships engaged in carrying passengers and goods between the British Islands and North America has of late years increased with wonderful rapidity. In 1864 no less than ten regular lines of ocean steamers were employed in running either to New York or to ports north of that City in the United States or Canada. Of these ten lines, two were weekly, and eight fortnightly, equivalent in all to six weekly lines, so that there were on an average six steamships, leaving each side weekly or nearly one every day.

'The total number of passengers carried by these various Steam lines during the past year was 135,317 and by far the largest number travelled in the summer months. It would not take a very large proportion of passengers crossing in one year to give employment to a *daily line* of *steamers* on the Short Ocean Passage route from St. John's to Valentia or Galway. A total number of 40,000 each way would give 200 passengers each trip for seven months of the year. It is obvious, then, that there is already abundance of passenger traffic, if the passenger route under discussion possesses sufficient attractions.'

Finally, Fleming concluded his argument with these words:

'If, as it has been shewn, this route would reduce the time between London and New York some three or four days, and bring Toronto one third nearer Liverpool (in time) than New York is now; if it be possible by this proposed route to lift the mails in London and lay them down in New Orleans in less time than they have ever reached New York, then it surely possesses advantages which must eventually establish it not simply as an inter-colonial, but rather as an Inter-Continental line of communication.

'There are purely commercial considerations, and however important they may be as such the Statesman will readily perceive, in the project, advantages of another kind. It may be of some consequence to extend to Newfoundland as well as to the other Provinces of British America, the benefits of rapid inter-communication. It will probably accord with Imperial Policy to foster the shipping of the Gulf and to encourage the building up of a Fleet of swift steamers as a daily line across the Ocean would require. It must surely be important to the Empire to secure in perpetuity the control of the great Highway between the two Continents. It must be equally her policy to develop the resources and promote the prosperity of these Colonies—and to bind more closely by ties of mutual benefit, the friendly relationship which happily exists between the people on both sides of the Atlantic.'

In these words Fleming put before the Canadian Government his ideas on communication between North America and Europe. Before studying the government's reactions, however, reference must be made to an important event which had taken place in 1864, while Fleming was still busy on his survey.

By the middle of the nineteenth century a few of the more imaginative leaders of the colonies in British North America had seen the vision of a single nation incorporating all the scattered settlements between Vancouver Island and Newfoundland. The scheme for an Intercolonial Railway on which Fleming was now engaged fostered this idea, with the feeling that all would benefit under some form of political and economic union. But the chief factor, perhaps, was the belief that only a strong transcontinental union could prevent encroachment and possibly eventual absorption by the expanding United States.

Maritime federation was already in the air, and in October 1864 the governments of Nova Scotia, New Brunswick and Prince Edward Island called a meeting in Charlottetown to discuss the matter. The provinces of Upper and Lower Canada asked to be allowed to attend the conference to state their views regarding the federation of all British colonies in North America. As a result of this meeting, discussions took place in Quebec and London culminating in the British North America Act of 1867 which created a union of four provinces: Quebec (formerly Lower Canada), Ontario (formerly Upper Canada) Nova Scotia and New Brunswick. This was the beginning of modern Canada.

The effect of this union on Sandford Fleming's schemes was twofold. Firstly, one of the earliest decisions of the new government, of which Sir John Macdonald became the first Prime Minister, was to push ahead with the construction of the Intercolonial Railway according to Fleming's recommendations. Fleming himself became Chief Engineer for its construction. Secondly, the movement towards federation prompted the Canadian Government to approach those colonies which were still independent in order to persuade them to confederate. Among these was Newfoundland, and the subject of that country's confederation was inevitably bound up with the intercontinental railway. With a population of only 100,000, Newfoundland could never hope to finance the building of a line such as Sandford Fleming visualised, either from public or private funds. The offer made by Sir John Macdonald was to find the cost of the railway and a steam ferry if, in return, Newfoundland would confederate with Canada. This, however, the Newfoundland Government were not prepared to do. At that time the country's biggest market for fish was the United States, and Newfoundland wished to continue this trade on her own terms. Confederation became a political issue on the island, and quite a bitter one. In 1869 an election was fought on this issue, and the party in favour of confederation was defeated. From then on, little more was heard of the subject and not until 1949 did Newfoundland finally become part of Canada. Any hope of building the Newfoundland section of an intercontinental railway faded. At its eastern end Sandford Fleming's scheme had been baulked.

The rest of his plan was developing rapidly however, for in 1871, while still engaged on the construction of the Intercolonial railway, he was asked by the Canadian Government to undertake the construction of an even greater scheme—the building of what was to become the Canadian Pacific Railway, a line linking the Intercolonial Railway with the Pacific Coast. It was the promise of such a line that persuaded the Pacific colony of British Columbia to join the Confederation. If ever a country was brought into being by the railway, that country is Canada. Anyone looking for evidence of the influence of railways on society during the nineteenth century would do well to examine Canadian history.

With two major schemes on his hands (the Canadian Pacific alone required $100,000,000 of capital) Fleming might have been excused for dropping his idea of an extension of the railway across Newfoundland. But this was an essential part of his grand plan, and in 1874 he took the matter up again with the Newfoundland Government on his own account. He asked for permission to make a survey for a possible route for the line, and offered to pay the cost of the whole operation himself.

The Newfoundland Government could hardly resist an offer like this, and in the summer of 1875 the survey began. Fleming could not superintend it personally—he was too committed with his other two projects—and it was carried out on his behalf by Mr. Alec Light and a staff of nine surveyors. Their object was to find a suitable route for a line from St. John's to St. George's Bay on the west coast, this being considered purely as a part of the projected Intercontinental Railway and having no reference to the local needs of Newfoundland. Thus the final route surveyed passed through the uninhabited centre of the island, following that which Cormack had traversed half a century before. It touched none of the centres of population outside St. John's.

The surveyors were formed into three parties, each consisting of a Chief Engineer, two Assistant Engineers, and 25–30 labourers, recruited locally. Party A surveyed the eastern side of the Avalon Peninsula, inland from St. John's. They then went round by sea to St. George's Bay, the most westerly point, and worked inland as far as the Exploits River. This was hard going; for eighty-five miles they had to cut a path through thick timber.

Party B had the central section, between the Gander and Exploits Rivers. One of their engineers, Mr. Costigan, travelled 120 miles by canoe along the Exploits River in the course of the survey. The third party, C, appears to have had the most difficult time. They had to start from the Avalon Peninsula and find the best practicable route through the interior to a point on the Gander River. This covered the most mountainous part of the route, the work was arduous, provisions ran short and there was insubordination among the labourers. The party had to turn back when fifteen miles short of the Gander River.

In general the survey was carried out successfully, however, and Sandford Fleming was able to report to the Newfoundland Government that he had found a satisfactory route across the island from St. John's to St. George's Bay for a railway of standard gauge (4 ft. $8\frac{1}{2}$ in.). For a single track, he estimated the cost at \$27,980 per mile with masonry works, and with timber works at \$25,988 per mile. For the distance surveyed, this would have worked out at six or seven million dollars for the whole scheme; a small matter compared with the hundred million of the Canadian Pacific Railway, but a large sum for a small colony like Newfoundland. The government were interested however; there was agitation in the country for railways to open up the interior, and prominent people, such as Bishop Mullock were pressing the point. Moreover, the country was now in a more prosperous state and more likely to be able to meet the cost of the necessary loans. It really looks as if Sandford Fleming's scheme might now succeed. But once again political considerations arose which blocked the realisation of his plan.

The difficulty this time arose from a matter of treaty rights. Throughout the eighteenth century the British and French had struggled for possession of Newfoundland and its valuable fishing grounds. In 1713 the sovereignty had passed to Britain, but by the Treaty of Utrecht of that year the British recognised the right of the

French to fish from the west coast of Newfoundland, the 'French Shore' as it became known, and there was a clause in the treaty which prohibited any permanent installation from being erected within half a mile of the foreshore, lest it should hinder the French fishermen from exercising their privileges. St. George's Bay, the western terminus of the proposed railway, was on the 'French Shore' and the building of the line would obviously infringe this right. The difficulty might have been overcome quite easily by negotiation, but unfortunately the Imperial Government were unwilling to pursue the matter, and would not give their approval to the building of the railway. As the Newfoundland Government depended on being able to raise the necessary capital in Britain, they had reluctantly to shelve the railway proposals, and once again politics overruled practical considerations.

After this set-back Fleming made no more attempts to extend his railway through Newfoundland, which meant the abandonment of his scheme for a short line to Europe. For the next ten years he was engaged in linking up the various colonies of British North America into what is now Canada. At 9 p.m. on November 7th, 1885, he was present at a little mountain station in British Columbia to see the last spike of the Canadian Pacific driven by D. A. Smith, the President of the Company. From that day the various provinces of Canada were linked by steel from the Atlantic to the Pacific, and the early dream of Sandford Fleming became a reality.

Before this had come about, Fleming was already looking for fresh worlds to conquer, as the following letter written by him reveals.

'The Pacific terminus of the Canadian Pacific Railway will in all probability be finally determined this year, and the telegraph now erected from Lake Superior and carried almost to the base of the Rocky Mountains will then be extended to the tidewaters of British Columbia. . . . If these connections are made we shall have a complete overland telegraph from the Atlantic to the Pacific Coast. It appears to me to follow that, as a matter of Imperial importance the British Possessions to the west of the Pacific Ocean should be connected by submarine cable with the Canadian line. Great Britain will thus be brought into direct communication with all the greater colonies and dependencies without passing through foreign countries.'

Thus did Sandford Fleming initiate another great project in which he was to play a leading part—the Pacific Cable, the All-Red Line, linking Canada with New Zealand and Australia. The letter quoted above was written by him to the Superintendent of the Telegraph and Signal Services of Canada—none other than Frederick Newton Gisborne, formerly manager of the New York and Newfoundland Electric Telegraph Co.—the man who started it all. History weaves some curious patterns in the affairs of man.

That might have been the end of the matter. But although Sandford Fleming abandoned his dream of a railway and steamship link with Europe, others now had the same idea. One more attempt was made, under very different circumstances, to put the idea into effect. It came about in this way.

In 1880 Newfoundland at last got its railway. In that year the government passed an act authorising the raising of money to be applied to building a railway from St. John's to Notre Dame Bay in the north of the island. This would be no Intercontinental, or even Intercolonial Railway; it would have no connection with the mainland, but was visualised as a narrow-gauge line linking the fishing communities of the north coast with the capital. On May 9th, 1881, the government entered into a contract with five persons, namely William Bond, Frank Allen, Celden X. Hobbs, Domingo Vasquez and Albert Blackman, to build a line of 3 ft. 6 in. gauge for 340 miles from St. John's to an inlet of Notre Dame Bay, called Hall's Bay. Construction of the line began on August 9th, 1881. It was, in the words of the Act, 'not of first-class construction'. The rails weighed only 35 lb. per yard; the bridges were of timber, and the first locomotives, built in England, were dainty little 10-ton tank-engines like the *A. L. Blackman* (Albert Blackman was attorney to the syndicate which was incorporated as the Newfoundland Railway Company).

Such a railway had little in common with Sandford Fleming's idea of a transcontinental line, epitomised in the C.P.R. which at that time was blasting its way through the Rockies. Instead, the Newfoundland Railway of 1881 was the sort of line which, if it existed in England today, would be the object of loving attention from a railway preservation society! But its directors had other ideas. On

May 20th, 1882, an Act was passed by the Newfoundland Legislature incorporating a company with the high-sounding title of the 'Great American and European Short Line Railway Company'. Its objects were stated as 'the establishment of more safe and speedy communication between America and Europe by way of Newfoundland'. The directors of the company were Mr. Albert Blackman and his associates, with the addition of two others. Among the powers granted to the company was that of taking over any existing lines in Newfoundland, which seems to indicate that the Newfoundland Railway, just a year old, and still only a few miles long, was to become part of a much bigger project.

The purpose of the new company, as stated in its act, was 'to construct a line from a point on the east or south-east coast of Newfoundland to a point on the west or south-west coast, to connect by ferry with a point on the eastern coast of Cape Breton and be worked in conjunction with lines of railway to be constructed by the company to the Straits of Canso, thence along the North shore of Nova Scotia to a point at or near Oxford, Amherst, or some other suitable point of intersection with the Intercolonial Railway of Canada; thence, through New Brunswick, and thence after passing through the State of Maine and other intervening states in the direction of Montreal, to a point opposite Montreal, with a branch to Quebec'.

The company was to have power to construct and to hold property in Maine (subject to the laws of that state) and its head office could be in New York, London or Newfoundland. The Newfoundland Government agreed to grant the necessary land to the extent of 100 feet from the centre of the track either way. Work was to begin within three years of the passing of the Act and to be finished within six years. An associated company, the 'Great American and European Express Company' having the same directors, was formed on the same day to act as common carriers and establish a parcels or packet express. The railway company had already been incorporated, under the same title, in Nova Scotia and in the Dominion of Canada.

Such was the final attempt to create a short-line route to Europe via Newfoundland. It was, alas, little more successful than the other attempts, though this time the difficulties were financial, not political. In 1883 work was started on that section of the line between Oxford Junction and New Glasgow, in Nova Scotia. Before it was completed, however, work was suspended, and the company having failed to pay the contractors for work done, all their property, rights, franchises, etc., were transferred to trustees for the contractors with power to sell such assets at public auction.

In June 1887 a Dominion Act authorised the Minister of Railways and Canals to acquire the incompleted works and property of the company, and to construct the line from Oxford Junction for sixty-two miles as a branch of the Intercolonial Railway, which now terminated at Halifax.

There is no known record of any activity by the company in Newfoundland. Indeed, after the statute of incorporation, the name never appears again, and the whole business is surrounded by an air of mystery. The Newfoundland Railway Co. continued in its original form until 1890, when it was bought up by the Newfoundland Government. The Great American and European Short Line Railway presumably disappeared when its rights lapsed in 1888.

So ended the last attempt to make Newfoundland the terminus of the great North American railway system. In due course the development of fast ships on the Atlantic route reduced the time between London and New York to such an extent that the short-line route of Sandford Fleming would have had little advantage. The idea faded into that corner of history devoted to unfulfilled visions, along with such schemes as the Channel Tunnel and the Cape to Cairo Railway. Today it is largely forgotten.

CHAPTER 6

The Reality—The Newfoundland Railway

ALTHOUGH THE SHORT ocean passage route from Europe to America via Newfoundland never became a reality in the sense in which Sandford Fleming visualised it—that is, as a direct, through passage between the two continents—it has been possible for many years for anyone who has wished to do so, and who has had the time to spare, to take a steamship from Liverpool to St. John's, a train across Newfoundland and a ferry to the mainland, and then to travel by Sandford Fleming's Intercolonial Railway to Montreal and all points west.

It is still possible for anyone to do it today; anyone, that is, who is not in a hurry and is prepared to spend ten days on the trip. As this book goes to press the closure of passenger services across Newfoundland have been announced. There is a regular steamship service from Liverpool to St. John's. The ships are freighters and carry few passengers, for Newfoundland is now only six hours by air from London. After a week at sea there is a railway trip across Newfoundland which takes a day, and the remainder of the journey to Montreal takes another two days.

To anyone with a liking for railways of an unusual kind, the ride across the island is easily the best part of the journey, for the line consists of a single narrow-gauge track which winds its way round tortuous curves, up and down seemingly impossible gradients, through a country which for most of the way is as wild as when Frederick Gisborne surveyed it for the first telegraph. In spring and autumn the train is sometimes held up for hours by herds of moose crossing the line, and in winter for days by snowdrifts in the way. Legends have grown up around the Newfoundland Railway, some based on fact, others more doubtful. All have become folklore by now. There is, for instance, the story of how the first locomotives were charged repeatedly by bull moose, until someone discovered that the engine whistles sounded like a bull moose's mating call. The note of the whistles was changed and all was well again. There is the story of the Battle of Foxtrap, between the inhabitants of that place and the engineers who were surveying the line; of which more later. Ghost trains have their place in the history of the railway, and there are countless stories of the type in which passengers alight from the train whilst in motion, pick strawberries, catch fish, shoot partridge or otherwise occupy themselves, and then catch up and board the train again.

Early in its history the railway had a curse put upon it by a Micmac Indian Squaw, when she discovered that some baskets she had left in a station yard had been damaged. That year the railway suffered the worst winter within living memory, and although the line has survived to this day, thus outliving many younger and apparently more vigorous enterprises, the curse is still remembered when trains run late or freight is lost. Those of us who have suffered in a like manner at the hands of railway companies in whatever part of the world must have a sneaking sympathy with that Indian squaw, though we may never have contemplated quite such drastic reprisals.

There is a strong flavour of the old Irish narrow-gauge lines about the Newfoundland Railway, which is hardly surprising in view of the fact that a large proportion of Newfoundlanders have ancestors who hailed from the Emerald Isle, and the Irish brogue is heard everywhere. It must have been a Newfoundland-Irish railway official who many years ago gave the instruction that at a passing place where space was limited, 'Engineers of all trains must bring their trains to a dead halt and wait until the other train has passed them'. Mixed up with all this is the fascination of a railway which traverses wild and remote places. Certainly nothing could be more unlike an intercontinental trunk line, but nevertheless it has a character all its own.

The history of the line really begins in 1879, in which year a Liberal government came into power under Sir William Whiteway, pledged to begin the building of a railway—not as a link with the mainland (that idea had been shelved)—but as a means of communication between the capital and the numerous outports along the northern coast, and also to develop mining and lumbering in the interior. A government commission of enquiry was set up, and their report, published in 1880, recommended a narrow-gauge line from St. John's to Hall's Bay, on the north coast, with branches to Harbour

Grace and Placentia. The purpose of this railway was set out very well in the closing paragraphs of the report which read as follows:

'We do not regard it per se as an enterprise that will pay, or as one that offers attractions to speculators, but as the work of the country, and in its bearing on the promotion of the well-being of the people, in which the returns are alone sought and will be found, it eminently commends itself to our judgement. In this sense we believe that in time it will amply pay its cost, and that the consequent advance in the comfort and independence of the people will fully attest the wisdom of its establishment.'

One would imagine that building such a line would be comparatively straightforward. By 1880 the technique of railway building was well advanced, with half a century of experience behind it. For the most part this railway would traverse virgin country; no questions of way-leave or property rights would arise. There were few roads to cross; the difficulties, in fact, were almost all natural ones. Yet the history of railway building in Newfoundland was one of endless set-backs, and it was nearly twenty years before the line was finished.

As with the Intercontinental Railway, the difficulties were both political and financial. The railway was always a political issue, and there were plenty of opponents ready to denounce it as a wild extravagance. The main financial difficulty was that of raising the necessary capital, and in their efforts to do this the government were led into decisions based on considerations of false economy, which put them at the mercy of people who too often turned out to be men of straw. Mistakes which many of the early railway builders in Britain and America had made many years before were repeated in Newfoundland.

The Government report of 1880 was the culmination of many years of public campaigning for a railway, beginning as far back as 1847 when a suggestion appeared in the press for a railway from St. John's to Portugal Cove, a place on Conception Bay, about eight miles from St. John's. In the succeeding years many prominent men in the island advocated opening up the country by rail. Among these was the Reverend R. Morris who published a pamphlet on the subject, and our old friend of the days of the telegraph, Bishop Mullock.

THE NEWFOUNDLAND RAILWAY

The survey by Sandford Fleming in 1875 also, of course, stimulated interest in the subject.

Once the recommendation to build a railway had been made, government action was swift. The commission reported in favour of the railway on April 2nd, 1880; on April 9th, exactly a week later, the Railway Bill had been published, and by April 19th it had been passed by the Legislature and had become law—a speed of action which would have been the envy of early railway promoters in Britain. The Act provided for the raising by loan of $25,000,000, the money to be applied to the building of a narrow gauge line of railway from St. John's to Hall's Bay, an inlet of Notre Dame Bay, on the north coast, with branch lines as required. A board of five 'Railway Commissioners' was to be appointed to carry this into effect.

The Commissioners met immediately and resolved to make a start on a railway between St. John's and Harbour Grace. Harbour Grace was at this time the second largest place in Newfoundland, and is situated about ninety miles from the capital on a peninsula between Conception Bay and Trinity Bay. It is not far from Heart's Content, where the Atlantic cable had been landed in 1866.* When the full length of railway had been completed, Harbour Grace would be the terminus of a branch line; but to begin with the Commissioners decided to survey the railway from Harbour Grace to St. John's as one project, extending the main line later.

The survey began on July 12th, 1880, and was carried out by the firm of Kinniple and Morris of London, working in two parties from opposite ends. On July 27th the eastern party ran into serious trouble at the village of Foxtrap, some ten miles out of St. John's. Members of the anti-railway group had been busy, working assiduously on the feelings of the local inhabitants. The railway, they said, would inevitably mean confederation with Canada. The little red flags which the surveyors were putting up along the route were Canadian flags; the land they crossed would be taken from its owners by the Canadian Government which would also tax everybody; when the railway was completed a toll-gate would be placed across the road to St. John's to force people to use the railway; and so on. So

---

* The reader will probably have noted by now that one of the more picturesque features of Newfoundland is the character of its place-names: Heart's Content and Harbour Grace are only two examples of a list which includes such titles as Bareneed, Blow-Me-Down, Topsails, St. Jones Without, Joe Batt's Arm and Come-by-Chance.

successful were these trouble-makers that almost the whole village turned out, men, women, and children, to bar the way of the surveyors. These unfortunate men, in spite of their protestations, were attacked, stoned, and beaten, and their flags and instruments taken from them. In his *History of Newfoundland* D. W. Prowse, who was a judge of the Central District Court of Newfoundland, describes the incidents following the 'battle' as follows:

'For five days the whole population from Topsail to Indian Pond were in an insane state of excitement. Though it was the busiest time of the year they never did a stroke of work; all day long they watched the engineers and the small posse of police and followed from from place to place. From Topsail to Indian Pond the whole population believed the advent of this terrible monster the railway meant their ruin.'

Although modesty prevents him from mentioning it in his book, it was Judge Prowse who was largely responsible for restoring order. Arriving from St. John's with Mr. Carty the Inspector of Police and a small force of armed constables, the Judge addressed the rioters after their ringleader had been arrested at the point of the bayonet. He did so with such effect that they were persuaded to give up the flags and theodolites which they had hidden in their houses, and to allow the engineers to continue peaceably with their work. The incident passed into Newfoundland folklore as 'The Battle of Foxtrap' and is still related with various embellishments. In one version the women of Foxtrap are said to have chased the luckless surveyors with pails of brine which they threw over them. While this would be very effective in the winter (the brine would remain liquid below freezing point), the accuracy of the report is doubtful, whatever one's opinion of Newfoundland weather, as the battle took place in July.

It is easy to smile at the gullibility of the people of Foxtrap, but one has only to think of Sandford Fleming and the connection between his proposed railway and confederation with Canada, and also to remember that, only five years before, Fleming's own engineers had conducted a survey, to see that there was some basis of fact on which the agitators could build their falsehoods. It was not just a case of a number of illiterate people being hoodwinked; at this time the Newfoundland people had a strong aversion to any suggestion of confederation. They had only recently (in 1855) achieved self-government and were in no hurry to give it up; Newfoundlanders are fairly independent people. Not until 1949 did they enter confederation, a step which has since proved of immense benefit to the country. Against this background however, it is easy to see how the trouble-makers were able to work on the feelings of the people of Foxtrap.

The survey of the line as far as Harbour Grace was completed in the summer of 1880, and the Railway Commissioners set about finding someone to build their railway, and here they erred badly. The more reputable contractors, such as Sir Hugh Allen who was at that time taking part in the building of the Canadian Pacific Railway, would naturally not tender for the whole line to Hall's Bay, but only for that part which had been surveyed, i.e., from St. John's to Harbour Grace. In their haste to press on with the work, the Commissioners entered into an agreement with a syndicate of New York businessmen who were prepared to contract to carry out the whole of the work without further survey. Their names have already been mentioned in a previous chapter: William Bond, Frank Allin, Celden Hobbs, Domingo Vasquez, and Albert Blackman. Albert Blackman was attorney to the syndicate. As we have already seen, this syndicate were not really interested in the motives of the Newfoundland Government in planning the railway, but had other ideas of their own. They wanted to build a railway across the island to link up with a projected line through the Maritime Provinces to Montreal—Sandford Fleming's original idea of an intercontinental line. This motive, however, did not become apparent until a year later.

By an Act of the Newfoundland Legislature dated May 9th, 1881, the syndicate were incorporated as 'The Newfoundland Railway Company', and the new company entered into an agreement (known as the 'Blackman Contract') with the government 'to locate, construct, equip, maintain, and continuously operate in an efficient and safe condition, as their sole property, 340 miles of railway in the island of Newfoundland from St. John's to Hall's Bay'. For their part the government agreed to grant 5,000 acres of land per mile, and promised a mail subsidy of $530 per annum for each mile of track, this to last for thirty-five years, at the end of which time the government would have the option of buying the railway. By the terms of the agreement the company were to build 'a substantial, reliable, and efficient railway (not of the first class)', of 3 ft. 6 in. gauge with steel rails of not less than 35 lb. per yard, and bridges of wood or iron. They were to provide at least six locomotives and six fully equipped trains (three passenger and three freight), and the passenger trains were to be operated at not more than forty miles an hour,* nor less than fifteen. The railway was to be in operation not later than five years from the date of the contract, a condition which was to prove of considerable importance in the future history of the line.

To carry out the construction of the line the company engaged as their contractors the firm of Davenport & Pierson of New York. By the terms of the contract work should have begun on August 9th, but it was not until a week later that work actually got under way— a beginning that did not augur well for the future. On August 16th work began at St. John's with fifty men opening up ground where the line swept in a curve around the northern edge of the city to enter from the east. The terminus was at Fort William, which in days gone by had been the headquarters of the military garrison, and from this depot a short spur line branched off towards the Narrows. Here the Railway Company had a pier close to Chain Rock, the point from which many years ago heavy chains had been hung across the harbour mouth to keep out the French warships.

By October 11th the pier was sufficiently complete to receive the first consignment of rails from Cardiff by the S.S. *Standard*. On December 5th the S.S. *Merlin* arrived from Nova Scotia with the first locomotive, which was put in steam immediately and used in constructing the line. This engine was 4–4–0 tank engine purchased second-hand from the Prince Edward Island Railway, which was also of 3 ft. 6 in. gauge. It was one of a number built for that line in 1872 by the Hunslet Engine Co. of Leeds, England. The Newfoundland Railway acquired five of them in all.

Work proceeded smoothly, and by the time winter halted construction ten miles of line had been metalled and work had begun from the Harbour Grace end. During the winter snows work was confined to cutting sleepers, though many of these were imported from Nova Scotia—a surprising feature of the construction, for

---

* As it turned out, there was little risk of this happening.

Newfoundland is plentifully supplied with black spruce which is quite adequate for the purpose. This particular form of sending coals to Newcastle was typical of the waste and mismanagement which prevailed throughout the building of the line and which was to bring about the downfall of the Railway Company.

Work was resumed in the spring, and in June a second locomotive arrived from England. This one, built by the Hunslet Engine Co. of Leeds, was the *A. L. Blackman* which has already been described (Chapter 5). Work on the construction of the line seems to have proceeded slowly during 1882, but two very important events took place during the summer. On May 20th a new company was incorporated by an Act of the Newfoundland Legislature. Under its grandiose title of the 'Great American and European Short Line Railway Company' it had already been incorporated in Nova Scotia, and as mentioned in Chapter 5, its object was no less than 'the establishment of more safe and speedy communication between America and Europe by way of Newfoundland'. This was to be accomplished by a line of railway (referred to in the company's prospectus as an 'air-line', though for no very obvious reason) from Montreal to Louisburgh, with a train ferry across to Newfoundland and a rail link to St. John's. It was, in other words, an attempt to fulfil Sandford Fleming's dream of a through route. The company proposed to buy 417 miles of railway already built or under construction in Nova Scotia and to build the remainder. Indeed, work had already begun in March on part of this between Oxford and New Glasgow, and now the company had applied for incorporation in Newfoundland, with a view to starting work on its proposed route across the island.

The Act of Incorporation provided for the grant of land by the Newfoundland Government to the extent of 100 feet on either side of the proposed line of the railway and also gave the new company powers to take over existing lines in Newfoundland.

All of this sounds a little odd when one recalls that the existing Newfoundland Railway Company had been incorporated only in the previous year. Even more astonishing, however, is the fact that the directors of the new company were the same syndicate that had formed the Newfoundland Railway Company: Albert Blackman and his associates! Having contracted to build a narrow gauge and purely local line, and having begun its construction, they were now asking to be allowed to convert it into a trunk line connected to the mainland—a totally different proposition. What is even more astonishing is that the Newfoundland Legislature should have agreed to this in principle and have passed the Act incorporating the new company, which would have the effect of so drastically changing their own plans.

It is fairly obvious that Blackman and his associates had entered into the railway contract the previous year without disclosing their real intentions. A narrow gauge line would be of little use to them if they wanted to run a train ferry carrying cars to the mainland, for the difference in gauges would make through working impossible. However, the contract gave them an opportunity to 'get a foot in the door', with a view to future developments. This opportunity they were now trying to make the most of.

The Newfoundland Government had, in fact, been 'taken for a ride' as they were soon to learn to their cost. The syndicate were not men of substance, and suffered from chronic impecuniosity. The whole idea of the 'Great American and European Short Line Railway' had a slightly insane air about it under the existing circumstances, and this became more obvious as time went on.

The other important event of the year was the action taken by the syndicate to raise additional capital for the Newfoundland Railway. Acting in accordance with the terms of their act of incorporation, in July 1882 they employed a firm of London bankers, Melville Evans and Co. to float a loan of £400,000 by the sale of £100 bonds at £98 each. These carried interest at 6 per cent. The security for this loan was a mortgage on the Southern Division (that is, the first 100 miles) of the railway itself. The company was in fact pledging the railway already built, and to a large extent unbuilt. The bonds, which were redeemable after thirty-five years, were all sold.

Thus fortified with additional capital the company proceeded to enlarge its supply of rolling stock. The six existing engines were joined by another seven, all from the well-known English firm of Hawthorn and Co. of Newcastle-on-Tyne. First came another little 10-ton, six-coupled, tank engine (a saddle tank this time); obviously intended for use as a contractor's engine and switcher. Then, for use in traffic, came four 2–6–0 tender locomotives with 13 in. × 18 in. cylinders. The first of these was named *St. John's*. Lastly, there were two 2–8–0 engines with 15 in. × 18 in. cylinders, presumably for freight work. Although built in England the tender engines were of typical North American design, with bar frames, cow-catchers, headlights, and spark-arresters. All these were supplied in 1882.

Another event of the year, though not perhaps of the same importance, was the first passenger excursion. On August 15th the Total Abstinence Society of St. John's organised an outing to Topsail, a seaside resort about eight miles from the city. This was in the area, where, two years before, the Battle of Foxtrap had taken place. On this occasion, however, there is no record of any hostility as the trainload of Total Abstainers rolled into Topsail behind the snorting *St. John's*.

Even with the additional capital from England the company did not make much progress with construction. There was mismanagement and waste, and money disappeared without much to show for it in return. Where it went will probably never be known, but the company were certainly not extravagant in the payment of wages. Letters in the press at this time complain of the difficulties experienced by workmen in collecting their wages. One man who had successfully sued the company for arrears complained that he still could not get the money in spite of the court decision. By the end of 1882 less than fifty miles of track had been laid; in fact the fiftieth mile was not reached until August 1883. This was made the occasion for a little ceremony, for on August 22nd the cruiser H.M.S. *Canada* was in St. John's harbour, and serving in her as a midshipman was Prince George, later to become His Majesty King George V. The President of the Newfoundland Railway Company, Mr. William Bond, who had recently arrived from New York, invited the ship's officers for a picnic trip on his railway. At the fiftieth mile, where construction work was going on, the future king drove in a ceremonial spike. Not until November 1st, 1884, was the line finally complete to Harbour Grace and on November 24th it was opened for traffic. There was only one train a day in each direction, and the eighty-four miles was covered in five and a half hours. The critics were not slow to point out that it was considerably quicker to go by horse and buggy to Portugal Cove and then across Conception Bay by boat.

Meanwhile the syndicate had been having trouble with their other project in Nova Scotia. After less than a year work on the Great American and European Short Line between Oxford and New

H

Glasgow was stopped. The syndicate were unable to pay the contractors. Work was resumed in 1884, but only for a short while. In April 1885, by an Act of the Nova Scotia Government, all the company's assets were transferred to trustees to be sold by auction on behalf of the contractors. In due course the Minister of Railways and Canals took over the line and completed it. The G.A. & E.S.L.R. had come to an untimely end.

In Newfoundland it was obvious also that the syndicate had shot their bolt. They had, with a great struggle, reached to Harbour Grace, but this was less than one-third of the line they had contracted to build, and their capital was now exhausted. The railway had barely started to earn money, and they had the interest on the bonds to pay each half year. They threw in the sponge and announced that they could do no more.

The critics of the railway policy were full of glee at the plight in which the government found itself. Although it was obvious that the company would now never fulfil the contract, the terms allowed them five years in which to do so, and until the five years were up the Newfoundland Government could do nothing. In the meantime their plans for a railway had been frustrated. In the press critics rang every variation on the theme of 'I told you so'. The St. John's *Evening Telegram* described the line as 'poorly constructed and with antedeluvian rolling stock', and had this to say about the affair.

'In 1880 a New York syndicate undertook to build 380 miles of railway between St. John's and Hall's Bay.

'They have now succeeded in building 100 miles of a third-class tramway to Harbour Grace at a cost of £245,000, that would not fetch £5,000 if put up for auction tomorrow.

'The aforesaid £245,000 having been advanced by a firm of London bankers and promoters who subsequently tried to recoup themselves for the loan they had placed by extracting as much of it as possible from the pockets of unsuspecting clergymen, widows, and orphans, the company has ever since been paying interest out of capital to pacify the same.'

More trouble was to follow. The interest payable to the bondholders on July 1st, 1885, could not be paid; presumably the company's capital was now exhausted. The English bondholders, unsuspecting or not, foreclosed on the mortgage, took possession of the Southern Division of the Railway (which included all that had been built), and Mr. Francis Evans, M.P., of Threadneedle Street, in the City of London, was appointed receiver. For the rest of its separate existence he ran the railway through his manager in Newfoundland, Captain Noble, until the line was finally taken over by the Newfoundland Government in 1897.

By the terms of the Blackman contract the government had agreed to pay an annual subsidy of $530 per mile, and to make a grant of 5,000 acres per mile, the subsidy and grant to apply as each section of five miles was completed. This they had done for the eighty-four miles that had been completed. But for their part the railway company had contracted to complete the whole line by April 20th, 1886. When that date arrived and it was obvious that the railway would never be finished by the company, the government ceased to pay them any more subsidy on the grounds that the contract had been broken.

Acting in the name of the Newfoundland Railway Company, the receiver and the trustees for the bondholders now brought an action against the government in the Newfoundland Supreme Court, to recover the arrears of subsidy payments and to settle the question of whether the subsidy should be paid or not. The proceedings occupied most of 1886, and eventually the court found in favour of the Railway Company and Bondholders. Thereupon the Newfoundland Government appealed to the Judicial Committee of the Privy Council in London. After a further hearing in that court the decision of the Supreme Court was upheld, but it was also decided that the Newfoundland Government had grounds for a counter-claim against the Railway for breach of contract.

Back to the Supreme Court went the action for the breach of contract to be heard. Not until 1897 was the matter finally settled by the purchase of the railway from its trustees by the government.

It is perhaps appropriate to mention here that during its early years the Newfoundland Railway Company occupied much of the time of the Newfoundland Courts in litigation, sometimes as plaintiff, sometimes as defendant. In the first year of its construction the Railway sued the owners of a steamship which had rammed their pier at Chain Rock, while they themselves were frequently being sued by property owners seeking compensation for alleged damage. The most frequent of these were cases brought by farmers whose cows had been run over on the line at night. Either the cows found that the track made a comfortable bed or else one is led to suppose that some farmers found this a convenient way of getting rid of their elderly cattle. Sometimes it was the Railway Company who suffered the most damage from these incidents. On one occasion in the summer of 1882 a train of flat trucks carrying construction workmen was being propelled by the engine towards the terminus at St. John's when it ran into a sleeping cow and all the trucks were derailed and overturned, two of the men being killed. The results of another such collision with a cow at the same place a few years later is shown in one of the accompanying illustrations.

The Newfoundland Government were learning the hard way that building railways was not an easy matter. In 1885 a new administration under Sir Robert Thorburn came into power, and they resolved to continue the railway themselves, treating it as a public work financed out of the colonial treasury and supervised by the Railway Commissioners. When work began in the spring of 1886 it was on another branch line to Placentia, a township on Placentia Bay on the south coast. It may be wondered why effort should have been diverted into another branch line instead of getting on with the main project, but the answer lies in politics. It was alleged that the line was built to secure the allegiance of the Honourable Members for Placentia. Certainly the building of the railway was surrounded by a certain aura of mystery. The enabling Act provided for the construction of an ordinary highroad, with no mention of a railway. The road was constructed, however, to the standards of grading and curvature required for a railway. After it had been completed, track was laid on it, and one morning the inhabitants of Placentia woke up to find that they had a railway. In the Legislature, however, government spokesmen insisted for some time that it was only a road.

Placentia was a French stronghold in the seventeenth century, and it is steeped in the history of the struggles between France and England throughout the eighteenth century. It also has a place in modern history, for during the second world war the warships carrying Winston Churchill and Franklin D. Roosevelt met in the calm waters of Placentia Bay, and there, surrounded by the pine-clad hills of Newfoundland, the Atlantic Charter was signed and decisions taken that were to alter the whole course of world history.

THE NEWFOUNDLAND RAILWAY 117

Even the Placentia Railroad had its part in this historic event, for Lord Beaverbrook, at that time Minister of Aircraft Production, was summoned by Churchill to take part in the discussions. Flying from England, he landed at Gander Airport and went down to Placentia by rail, travelling in the caboose of a freight train to save waiting for the passenger train.

The Placentia Branch, twenty-five miles long, was completed in 1888, and the Railway Commissioners then continued with the main line. The work proved so costly, though, that it was given up when sixteen miles had been completed. Even under government construction the money still melted away.

There were now two railways in the island—one from St. John's to Harbour Grace via Whitbourne, owned and operated by the English investors, through a receiver, and known now as the Harbour Grace Railway, and the other from Whitbourne to Placentia, owned and operated by the Newfoundland Government. The two systems were joined physically at Whitbourne, having the same gauge, but in many other respects they differed. The Harbour Grace *Railway* had a distinctly English flavour, and all the locomotives were English. The Placentia *Railroad* on the other hand had its motive power (all two of them) supplied by Baldwins of Philadelphia, and the flavour was correspondingly North American.

In 1889 Sir William Whiteway's administration returned to power. He was determined to finish the building of the railway, and in June of that year an Act was passed authorising the raising by loan of $4,250,000 for that purpose. Tenders were called for, and this time more care was exercised in choosing the contractor. After much consideration the contract was awarded to Mr. (later Sir) Robert Reid of Montreal and his partner Mr. G. H. Middleton.

Robert Reid was a Scot, a contemporary of Sandford Fleming under whom he had worked on contracts for the Canadian Pacific Railway. In his youth he had emigrated from Scotland to Australia where he worked as a stone mason. From there he went to Canada, where he built up a considerable reputation as a bridge and railway contractor, as well as a considerable fortune. Later in life he became a director of the C.P.R. and of the Bank of Montreal, and was knighted.

In June 1890 Reid and Middleton contracted with the Newfoundland Government to build the remainder of the railway to

Hall's Bay within five years, for $15,000 per mile. In addition they agreed to take over from the government the operation of the Placentia Railroad. The Harbour Grace Railway continued to be operated by its receiver as a separate concern. For the first time the construction of the railway appeared to have been placed in competent hands. Work proceeded apace, and as if in earnest of its intention the new line was given the title of 'Hall's Bay Railway'. In 1892 Middleton dropped out of the partnership and Reid and his three sons continued on their own. By 1893 the railway had been extended 192 miles to a point known as Norris Arm, about 80 miles short of Hall's Bay. It now became apparent that for the railway to be of the maximum benefit to the country it ought to be extended to some point from which communication could be made with the mainland of Canada. Accordingly, the government decided that instead of terminating at Hall's Bay, the line should be diverted and continued to Port-aux-Basques in the south-west corner of Newfoundland, whence a ferry service of steamships could connect with Cape Breton. Thus Sandford Fleming's plan would be fulfilled, except that the route would be far less direct owing to the necessity of serving the many communities along the north coast.

A new contract was made with Reid, and in return for £1,000,000 sterling in debentures he agreed to extend the line the remaining 293 miles to Port-aux-Basques. The Hall's Bay Railway was renamed the Newfoundland Northern & Western Railway, a description of its new character. On the same day another contract was signed by which Reid agreed to operate the Northern & Western Railway and the Placentia Railroad for a period of ten years. In return he was granted 5,000 acres of land in fee simple for every mile of line operated.

The first of these two contracts was fairly comprehensive and gives a good idea of the line. It was to be a single-line track, of 3 ft. 6 in. gauge of course, laid with 50-lb rails on sleepers 7 ft. long, the sleepers being 2 ft. apart between centres. Water stations were to be provided every fifteen miles. The contractor was to provide five locomotives; two 4–4–0 or American type; two 2–6–0 or Mogul type; one 2–8–0 or Consolidation type. The rolling-stock was to include three first-class cars, one first- and second-class composite car, two second-class cars and three sleeping cars, as well as an official private car.

THE NEWFOUNDLAND RAILWAY 119

Freight vehicles to be supplied consisted of two mail and baggage cars, ten box-cars, thirty flat cars, a conductor's van, and a flanger car. Four snow ploughs completed the list. All were to be fitted with Westinghouse brakes. By the terms of the contract the minimum speed of trains was to be 18 miles an hour. This time no maximum speed was specified.

The railway builders changed the direction of their efforts to the south-west and the original objective of Hall's Bay was by-passed and left some thirty miles to the north. The going should now have been easier, as nearly all the rivers in Newfoundland run northwest or south-west. Instead of crossing the waterways the line would now be able to follow them. It took another six years, however, to complete the 293 miles to Port-aux-Basques, which the railway at last reached in June 1898.

On Wednesday, June 29th, the great moment arrived when the first overland express left St. John's. The passengers consisted of fifty ladies and gentlemen, most of them en route to a conference at Halifax, and on this Wednesday evening there was a large crowd at Fort William station to see them off. In Newfoundland the beginning of a journey is always an occasion, and whether by ship, railway, or airways, there is always a good assembly of friends and relations to see the travellers off. On this occasion there was the added interest that the journey represented the culmination of eighteen years' effort to complete an overland route to the mainland.

At 7 p.m. the first overland express pulled out of St. John's. It consisted of five vehicles: one baggage car, one day coach, a dining car, and the two sleeping cars *Placentia* and *Trinity*, under the charge of Conductor Stephen Howlett. Particulars of the locomotive have not been recorded, but it was probably one of the two 4–6–0 locomotives newly acquired from Baldwins and named *Sir Herbert Murray* and *Hon. Robert Bond* after the Governor and the Prime Minister of that date.

Engines and crews were changed at Clarenville (131 miles), Bishop's Falls (267 miles), and Humbermouth (413 miles). Port-aux-Basques was reached at 10.45 p.m. on June 30th, the journey of 541 miles having taken 27½ hours. The S.S. *Bruce* was waiting to take the travellers on the sea passage to Sydney. Newfoundland had at last been linked by rail with the mainland.

On the last stage of this trip the locomotive was in charge of

Engineer Joseph Burns whose lifetime spanned an era in the history of the railway. He lived to see the last steam locomotive in Newfoundland driven to its resting place in Bowater Park, near Cornerbrook, in 1956. There it stands today, a memorial to the men who drove the railway through the wildernesses of the Newfoundland interior and to the train crews who worked over this difficult line in the days of steam, often undergoing great hardships in the process of keeping the trains rolling.

On March 3rd, 1898, a few months before the first train had run, the Newfoundland Government had signed a new contract with Mr. Reid. By this he agreed to operate the whole railway system, including the Harbour Grace line, which had just been bought from the bondholders by the government, for fifty years. In return he was granted a further 5,000 acres of land a mile. A new line into St. John's was to be built, with a terminus at the western end of the harbour. The old line to the Fort William depot was then to be abandoned. (It later became a road, and is now known as Empire Avenue.) The depot itself caught fire and burned down in 1903.

These new grants of land made Robert Reid the owner of 4,124,200 acres of land which must have put him amongst the largest landholders in the world. Inevitably the contract came in for criticism; in the 1900 elections one of the rallying cries of the critics was 'Reid even owns our graveyards'. As well as his millions of acres he owned the street-car (tramway) system of St. John's, the port's only dry dock, was lessee of the entire railway system and of the country's telegraph system. Whatever one many think of monopolies, however, there is little doubt that without Reid and his capital few of the projects he operated would ever have existed.

That aspect of the contract which aroused most criticism, though, was the arrangement that on the completion of the railway Reid should pay $1,000,000 and at the end of fifty years the ownership of the railway should pass to him.

In 1901 Reid decided that his business, of which he was still the sole owner, would be better organised as a joint stock company. In return for the necessary Act of Incorporation he had, however, to give up his option on the line and receive back his $1,000,000, the new government that had come into power insisting on this condition. The railway now came under the operation of the Reid Newfoundland Company Ltd until 1923, when at the request of the company the

Newfoundland Government took over the operation, and from then on ran it as a government railway. The final change of operator came in 1949 when, on the entry of Newfoundland into confederation with Canada, the railway system was absorbed into the Canadian National Railways.

Today, travellers by rail from St. John's to the mainland begin their journey from Robert Reid's station at the west end of the harbour. The main building is of granite in Scottish Baronial style, a reminder that Reid brought many of his railway builders, especially stone-cutters and masons, from his own homeland. The names Cobb, Campbell, Henderson, Burton, Graham, and Ross are familiar in the history of the railway, and places along the line are named after some of them. Their work remains today in the form of the many culverts, bridge piers, and bridge abutments, all of granite ashlar from quarries along the line, and all of the high standard of workmanship one would expect from Scottish masons.

There is a regular daily airline service from St. John's to Halifax, but during the summer months many travellers, especially tourists, still prefer to make the journey by rail. So, from the middle of June to the middle of September, an express train, the *Caribou*, makes the overland crossing in each direction on six days a week. For the rest of the year passenger traffic is only sufficient for three trains a week. On days when the express does not run, those who wish to travel to places along the line (for many of which the railway is the only link with the outside world) must go by mixed train, which means two coaches attached to the rear of a freight. These coaches are of a type which make up into sleepers at night, and have a buffet at one end. Each coach thus provides all the requirements of comfortable travel. This is very necessary, as the journey is inevitably a leisurely one, with up to fifty-one stops en route; Port-aux-Basques being reached in $30\frac{1}{2}$ hours, 3 hours more than the first train took in 1898. Much of this time is spent, of course, in taking up and putting down freight.

In contrast, the Caribou does the journey of 547 miles in 23 hours —an improvement of $4\frac{1}{2}$ hours on the original timing, and a performance which is extremely good in view of the difficult route and the fact that there are thirty-one stops and many more 'flag' stops.

The *Caribou* usually consists of about ten cars: baggage and mail cars, day cars, two diners, and three or four sleepers. Sleeping cars are divided into sections, each of which contains two armchair seats and one upper and one lower sleeping berth at night. At one end of each car is a 'drawing room' or private two-berth compartment. Traditionally, cars are named after places on the island: 'Placentia,' after the bay of that name, 'Fogo', after an island on the north coast; 'Trinity' after the bay of Atlantic cable fame, and so on.

In their dark green livery, with broad yellow waist-band, the rake of cars making up the train presents a very smart appearance. In size and shape they are very similar to British main line stock, unlike the carriages of the early days which had the typical North American clerestory roof with rounded ends, and vertically boarded sides. At the head of the train will be one, or depending on the size of the train two, of the fifty-six diesel-electric locomotives introduced in the 1950–56 period. These are of the road-switcher type. They are built to the maximum loading gauge, for there are no tunnels on the Newfoundland Railway, and only a few overbridges of modern construction.

Today the arrival or departure of a train is still a social occasion. The single platform of the station is filled with a crowd of friends and relatives waiting to see passengers off or to greet arrivals. News of the progress of a cross-country train is broadcast over the local radio, along with the movements of aircraft and shipping, while travellers from other parts of the island, or from the mainland, may find their arrival chronicled in the local newspapers. All of which produces an element of drama in the daily arrival or departure of trains which lends pleasure to travelling, and gives an atmosphere very different from the impersonal business of moving commuters in and out of larger cities.

When the train starts with a jerk of couplings, and bumps over the switches as it crawls through the station yard with the locomotive bell clanging, any resemblance to a main line disappears and there is no doubt that one is on the narrow gauge. Straightway the line starts to climb away from its terminus almost at tide-water level. The passenger soon gets a vivid impression of the difficulties that had to be surmounted in building a railway through very broken, rocky, and mountainous country, much of it practically unknown. Great credit is due to the engineers who performed what was, after all, an engineering feat of considerable magnitude. It had been proposed to build the railway to a maximum curvature of 10 degrees and a maximum grade of 2 per cent.* This was too difficult to maintain, however, in the rugged territory encountered, and consequently on the western half of the line grades reached $2\frac{1}{2}$ per cent and curvature between 12 and 14 degrees. There are over thirty-five miles of track between 2 per cent and $2\frac{1}{4}$ per cent grade, and one mile at over $2\frac{1}{2}$ per cent. Curves of 10 and 12 degrees are common on some of the steepest grades. Train crews will tell one: 'Sometimes your train is going uphill and downhill at the same time, and round three curves all at once.'

The first sixty miles or so is in country inhabited in small villages scattered along the line. At Holyrood the line describes a huge horseshoe curve to skirt an inlet, and the whole length of the train can be seen from the carriage window. Whitbourne is passed, the former junction for the Harbour Grace line, re-routed to the east many years ago. Before the new depot at St. John's was opened in 1903, Whitbourne was the operating centre for the eastern half of the railway system.

The line traverses the narrow isthmus that joins the Avalon Peninsula to the rest of Newfoundland, and to the right and left can be seen respectively the Bays of Trinity and Placentia. A few miles farther on the line skirts Bull Arm where in 1858 the *Niagara* landed her half of the cable.

From here onwards the country is wilder and much more sparsely populated. Forests of black and red spruce, with occasional birch, are interspersed by marshes and lakes (known in Newfoundland as ponds, whatever their size). Pools of water shine brilliantly with white and yellow water-lilies, and all around them grow bushes of blueberries, cranberries, marshberries and the scarcer and much-prized bake-apple, which makes a very delectable preserve. Wild flowers grow in profusion, and prominent among them is a variety of the pitcher plant which lives upon the insects that it traps in its cup. Queen Victoria chose a pitcher plant to appear as an emblem

---

* In American and Canadian practice curvature is measured in degrees, that is, the angle subtended at the centre by a chord of 100 feet. Thus, the shorter the radius, the greater the angle. Gradients are usually measured in percentages, i.e. a gradient of 1 in 50 is described as a 2 per cent grade.

on Newfoundland's first coinage. She might have chosen a wild rose, for these are almost as common.

Frequent outcrops of rock indicate how shallow is the depth of soil, and from time to time the railway crosses brooks and streams which thread their way through and over the rocks. These abound in trout, and in the early and more leisurely days of the railway's existence, 'trouters' trains' were run during the holiday season. Setting out in the early morning they travelled some fifty miles out from St. John's, stopping at each stream or pond to set down a quota of sportsmen; and in the evening returned to pick up the fishermen and their catches. Travelling by train in Newfoundland is always a very sociable experience, and it is not difficult to imagine the experiences and yarns that must have been swopped as the 'trouters' train' rolled along on its way home.

From time to time the railway passes through remote country stations consisting of a single wooden building, with perhaps a passing loop and occasionally a couple of spurs of rusting rails running off into the surrounding woods where, unseen, they join to form a triangle on which locomotives can run round their trains.

Clarenville, 131 miles from St. John's, marks the end of the first operating section. It is reached in five and a half hours and there is a short halt while engine crews are changed. In the days of steam, locomotives were changed here also.

The line is single track throughout, with passing loops at intervals. Switches are operated by a trainman who travels with one. There are no signals, and control is by telegraph and passing order, with two control centres at St. John's and Bishop's Falls.

Eighty miles from Clarenville the train enters Gander, passing close by the great international airport. In foggy weather when flying from St. John's to Gander is restricted, the railway provides a useful alternative. It also brings in aviation fuel and stores.

Eleven hours and 260 miles from St. John's the *Caribou* arrives at Bishop's Falls, a town lying on the Exploits River, which is crossed just before entering the town by a long steel truss-bridge. With its neighbouring town of Grand Falls, Bishop's Falls forms a centre for the paper-making industry carried out by the Anglo-Newfoundland Development Company. It is also a railway centre, the Assistant Superintendent, Bishop's Falls, being responsible for the operation of the western half of the railway system, which one is about to enter. There are quite extensive railway installations; yards, locomotive sheds, and sidings. During a half-hour wait train crews are changed, the train serviced, and dining car stocks made up.

Leaving Bishop's Falls the line turns towards the north-west and begins to climb towards a high plateau which is crossed at a height of 1,700 feet. This area, known as the Topsails, is the most desolate and hazardous part of the whole line. For nearly fifty miles the railway runs through barrens: an area of tundra where no trees grow. The only vegetation is lichens and short, scrubby bushes. Jagged peaks of rock rear out of the ground at intervals, and it is the three largest of these (known respectively as the Gaff Topsail, Main Topsail, and Mizzen Topsail from their resemblance to a ship's sails) that give the area its name.

Even in summer the Topsails has a grim and forbidding appearance; at night, under a full moon, the traveller pulling aside his curtain and peering through the window from his comfortable sleeping berth might well imagine that he was gazing at another world; a lunar landscape, or some invention of science fiction. But in winter the desolation of the place is increased tenfold when north winds, sweeping down over Labrador from the Arctic Circle bring snow that piles up into drifts as much as fourteen feet deep, turning the barrens into a howling wilderness of white. Then, in spite of all efforts to keep the line clear, trains become stuck in snowdrifts for days at a time, while maintenance gangs work under appalling conditions to free them. To meet such contingencies trains carry emergency stocks of food and fuel, and train crews have been known to carry snowshoes!

Up on the Gaff Topsails, in the middle of this desolation, is a station known as Quarry. Here, in 1911, two station agents, George Hardy and William Boyd, carried out their duties turn and turn about. One night, the one on duty heard the sound of a train approaching from the east. It was a moonlit night, and looking through his window he saw a train of box-cars approaching, drawn by a high-funnelled locomotive. Its old-fashioned oil headlamp shone out in front, and behind it the plume of steam and smoke stood out in the moonlight as it drifted away over the barrens. In the words of an old railroad song:

'When she hove in sight far up the track
She was working steam with the brakeshoes slack,
She hollered once at the whistle-post,
Then flitted by like a frightened ghost;
He could hear the roar of the big six-wheel,
And her drivers pound on the polished steel,
And the screech of her flanges on the rail,
As she beat it west on the desert trail.'

The agent was puzzled, for he had received no warning of this train, and he signalled it to stop. But there was no response to his signals, and the train swept through the station. It was too dark to see the engineer, but as the train passed him the railwayman caught a glimpse of the number ten on the side of the dome and on the tender, before the train disappeared into the darkness, its red tail light glowing and dying away. He sent a telegraph message ahead to Howley to warn them of the approaching freight, then another irate message back to Millertown to report the train of which he had not been informed.

There was a short delay, then back came the reply that no train had been despatched. In fact, there wasn't a train within a hundred miles of Quarry. What did he mean?

By now the agent's anxiety was aroused, and when some time later Howley came on the line to ask where the freight was, as it had not appeared, it was obvious that something very strange had happened.

In the meantime all traffic was suspended until a pilot engine from Millertown had cautiously traversed the desolate stretch of line to Howley. There was no sign of the mysterious freight train which seemed to have vanished without trace.

There are, of couse, no such things as ghost trains, and when the authorities received the report of the incidents they no doubt attributed the unfortunate man's mistake to the strain of working in such a lonely post. One thing may have puzzled them however—there was no such engine as number ten. The only one of that number had come to a sudden end when its boiler burst near St. John's some years before. The engineer and the fireman had been killed.

In 1928 it was proposed to eliminate the Topsails area by diverting the railway farther south from Millertown Junction to Howley by way of Buchans. This would have made a longer way round, but avoided the barrens. Work was commenced, but when six miles had been completed the economic depression stopped further work, and in 1929 the track was taken up again. Since taking over the line in 1949 the C.N.R. have tackled the problem by raising the whole length of track over the barrens by as much as seven feet, thus making it easier to keep it clear of snow.

Descending from the plateau the line turns south and runs along the line of the Humber River and alongside Deer Lake, a stretch of very lovely country which forms a vivid contrast to the desolation of the barrens. The floor of the valley is farming country and pleasant pasture, while on either side the hills are covered with pine forests. It is not difficult to imagine oneself passing through the Trossachs, in Scotland. Farther down the valley, towards Cornerbrook, birch and maple trees grow profusely and in the autumn produce a mass of brilliant colours.

Just before it leaves Deer Lake the railway skirts Bowater Park, a pleasant recreation ground among the woods on the lake shore. There, by the side of the track, stands No. 593, last of a long line of steam locomotives to run in Newfoundland. Though relatively modern (she was built in 1920) she has an interesting genealogy, being descended from the first Pacific type locomotive in the world. This was designed by the New Zealand Railways engineering staff for use in that country, which, like Newfoundland, has a 3 ft. 6 in. system. The first locomotives to this design were built by Baldwins of Philadelphia in 1907. In 1920 the Newfoundland Railway ordered six locomotives from Baldwins, and these were supplied to the New Zealand design. One of them, No. 193, later became C.N.R. No. 593 and now rests under its log-built shelter in Bowater Park.

A few miles farther on the train enters Cornerbrook, a thriving town centred around Messrs. Bowaters' paper factory, the largest integrated pulp and paper mill in the world. As a contrast to the remoteness of the forests and barrens the train threads its way through huge industrial installations and past busy wharves where ships from all over the world load their cargoes of newsprint.

Cornerbrook marks the beginning of the last section of the line. Engine crews change, and the train is away again on the remaining 142 miles of its journey. Leaving the Humber estuary and striking inland the railway traverses mile upon mile of spruce forests—the raw material that feeds the Cornerbrook mills.

Towards the end of the journey the line runs along a coastal plain between the sea and the Long Range Mountains. From one of these, Table Mountain, the wind sweeps down in winter at speeds of up to 140 miles an hour. Whole trains have been known to have been swept off the rails here, and in former days it was the practice, when the wind reached a certain strength, to halt trains and chain them down to the track, the rolling stock being specially fitted for this purpose. Since the railway has been operated by the C.N.R. a retired sectionman has been employed to give warning of high winds. Stationed at Wreck House, at the point where the worst winds are encountered, he can telephone warning when wind speed reaches a certain level, and train services are then suspended and trains held outside the danger area until conditions improve.*

A final run along the edge of the coast, past mile after mile of golden sand, and the train enters Port-aux-Basques. Drawing into the freight yard, on one side of the harbour, it then sets back slowly round the triangle and into the passenger terminal on the other side of the harbour. The terminal is a modern building adjoining the jetty at which the motor vessel *William Carson*, modern equivalent of the S.S. *Bruce*, waits to transport its passengers to the mainland.

For more than half a century the railway was the only land route crossing Newfoundland. Then in 1962, the easternmost section of the Trans-Canada Highway was completed from Port-aux-Basques to St. John's. In August of that year it was inaugurated by a motor cavalcade which began from the Newfoundland end by dipping its wheels in the water of the Atlantic near St. John's, and then made its way across Canada to dip those same wheels in the Pacific. For most of its way the highway follows the railway, but is less direct. The railway is still kept busy, and many motor trucks and private cars still cross the island by rail, mounted on 'flats'.

Whatever may happen to railways elsewhere, the future of the Newfoundland Railway is assured for many years to come. There is talk that one day it may even be rebuilt to standard gauge. When that happens it will lose much of its unique character which for three-quarters of a century has caused Newfoundlanders to regard it with a mixture of amusement and affection. But that is the price of progress.

* This 'human wind gauge', as he was known, Mr. Lauchie MacDonald, died at Wreck House on Dec. 14th, 1965.

24 Bowater Pulp and Paper Mills, Cornerbrook

25. Cabot Tower, Signal Hill, St. John's, Newfoundland

26 Wireless apparatus used in early experiments by Sir Oliver Lodge

27 Thornycroft Steam Bus used by Marconi as a mobile wireless receiver

28 The Poldhu transmitter

29 Circular Aerial Array, Poldhu

30 Fan-shaped Aerial Array, Poldhu, in 1901

31 Marconi with his assistants, Kemp and Paget, at Cabot Tower

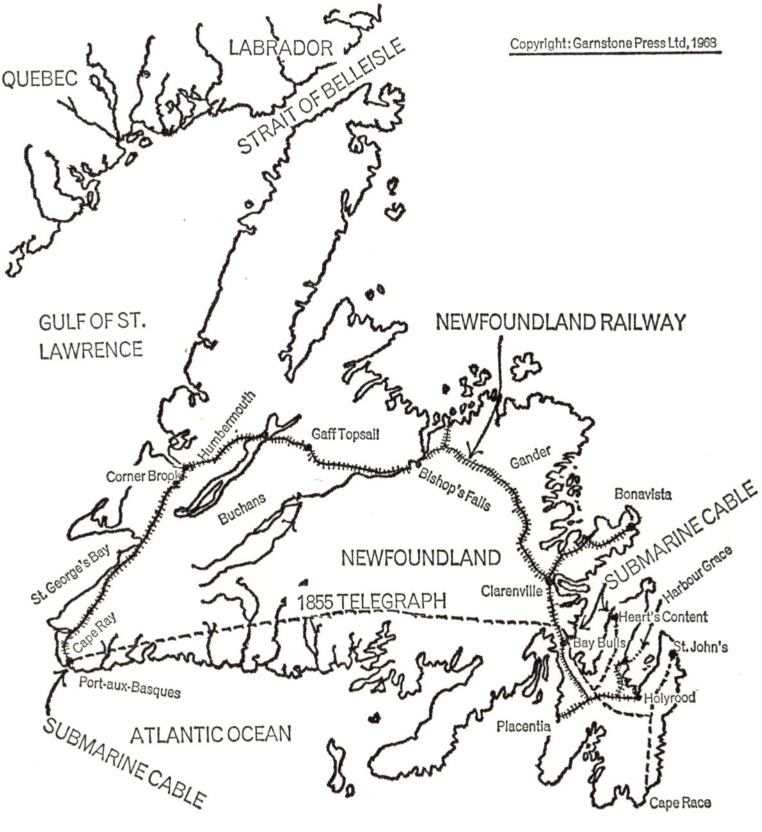
Copyright: Garnstone Press Ltd, 1968
QUEBEC
LABRADOR
STRAIT OF BELLEISLE
GULF OF ST. LAWRENCE
NEWFOUNDLAND RAILWAY
Humbermouth
Gaff Topsail
Corner Brook
Bishop's Falls
Gander
Bonavista
Buchans
SUBMARINE CABLE
NEWFOUNDLAND
Harbour Grace
St. George's Bay
Clarenville
1855 TELEGRAPH
Heart's Content
Cape Ray
Bay Bulls
St. John's
Port-aux-Basques
Holyrood
Placentia
ATLANTIC OCEAN
SUBMARINE CABLE
Cape Race

PART THREE
MARCONI AND HIS WIRELESS

CHAPTER 7

The First Transatlantic Wireless Message

ST. JOHN'S HAS one of the finest natural harbours in North America. About a mile long, and a third of a mile wide, it is almost completely landlocked. At its western end it is fed by the Waterford River. To the north, where the ground slopes gradually down to the water, is the city. Not very long ago this side of the harbour consisted of a motley collection of wharves and jetties, but these have now been replaced by a broad esplanade and sea-wall, to which ships can make fast and along which vehicles can pass, as at Langelinie in Copenhagen, making a waterfront worthy of the oldest city in North America.

To the south and east, hills rise straight out of the water to a height of 400 feet, and shelter the harbour from the fury of Atlantic gales. The easternmost hill is Signal Hill, and between it and the South-Side Hills lies the Narrows—a gap 700 feet wide in the solid rock, giving a passage to the Atlantic deep enough to take the largest ship. From the top of Signal Hill one has a magnificent view; to the east the great Atlantic; to the west the harbour and city in panoramic view; while below, on the south side of the hill, is the Narrows, so close that one feels one could throw a stone into the water. Such a commanding position has obvious military advantages and it is not surprising that from the early days of the colony fortifications were built on it. In the eighteenth century, during the wars between England and France, it changed hands several times before the French were finally defeated in 1762 by a British force under the command of Colonel Amherst. Following this victory Signal Hill was heavily fortified with several batteries of guns in strategic positions. Only one of these now remains: the Queen's Battery with its ancient guns still overlooks the Narrows from its commanding site just below the crest of the hill. Below it can be seen Chain Rock, from which, during the French Wars, a huge chain was stretched across the Narrows to Pancake Rock on the south side.

The chain could be hauled taut by tackles to prevent the entry of French ships.

Chain Rock and Pancake Rock reverted to their old use during the Second World War, when an anti-submarine net was suspended from them.

In addition to these fortifications, in 1795 a blockhouse was erected at the summit of Signal Hill. From it, watchers had a view of ships approaching St. John's when they were still some miles out to sea. After the danger of war had passed, and throughout the nineteenth century, the blockhouse on Signal Hill became adapted to peaceful purposes as a look-out and signal post. By means of it, signals could be exchanged between those in the city below and ships out at sea, and every merchant in St. John's had his own house flag and code number which he used in communicating with his ships via Signal Hill. On certain occasions during the year Signal Hill was the scene of tremendous excitement, as, for example, when the return of the sealing fleets from the spring seal-catching was expected. A graphic description of one of these scenes in about the year 1860 has been left by an eye-witness.

'Scarcely daybreak on the hill-tops; the merchants, wrestling for glasses and watching the fleet some miles off (chary of the ice-bound coast), lay heavily on the first ship past Fort Amherst, the number of her catch of seals and the house she may belong to. There is one vessel at least two miles further in than her consorts, her number is flying from her peak, but they cannot quite make it out. Ah, what palpitation! What tantalisation! The top flag is two, the lowest is a seven—no, it is a nine—which is it, Bowring's or McBride's? For it is clear that it is one of the twain. The schooner yaws for a second, but that's enough; the numbers stand out bravely in the breeze, and John Bowring, jumping up, shouts to the signal man to hoist the number of his house. Look over the Queen's battery, across the harbour, among the still hazy wharves and ships. Almost in less time than it can be written looms out a puff of white smoke, and to the faint boom of a gun the signal flag of the house on their own wharf is run up in acknowledgement of the joyful news. In ten minutes more they know that 7,000 seals are in the schooner's hold, and honest John, with crushed hat, flushed cheeks, and well-bespattered clothes, comes tearing down the hill, heeding nothing as he rushes past to his counting house. He knows that he has driven that last nail into his future villa on the banks of the Mersey. Good, honest, fellow! No one jealous of his luck; and yet few would take him for a partner at our whist club in the evening; his revokes would be something awful.'

The Block House on the summit of Signal Hill lasted until 1897. In that year it was replaced by a new signal tower, the Cabot Tower, built to commemorate the 400th anniversary of the discovery of Newfoundland by John Cabot. It is a rugged building of granite which seems almost to be part of the rock on which it stands. It was built by those same Scottish masons who worked on the railway, and they built it to withstand the force of the Atlantic gales for many years. Today it is a museum, for its original purpose as a signal tower was superseded by an invention of the twentieth century; an invention which curiously enough had its first major success on Signal Hill itself, in the Cabot Tower. Here, in December 1901, Guglielmo Marconi received the first message to be sent by wireless telegraphy across the Atlantic. He chose Newfoundland for the same reason that Cyrus Field did for his submarine cable, and Sandford Fleming for his intercontinental railway: it is the nearest point to Europe on the American continent.

To start at the beginning of the story we must go back to 1864, two years before Cyrus Field had finally succeeded in landing the cable at Heart's Content. In that year the Scottish physicist James Clerk Maxwell first propounded his theory of electromagnetic waves.

Maxwell was a contemporary and fellow-countryman of Professor Thompson of Atlantic cable fame. Like him, he was also something of an infant prodigy (both of them matriculated at the age of 12). After completing his education at Edinburgh University, Maxwell went to Cambridge as Professor of Experimental Physics. While there he produced, by mathematical reasoning, his theory that the effects of any electrical change, such as the stopping or starting of an electric current, should be to cause electromagnetic waves to spread outwards in space with a velocity equal to that of light.

This was a remarkable deduction, but at that time no means of producing or detecting such waves were known and Maxwell was unable to carry out any experiments to prove the truth of his theory. Not until 1888, twenty-four years laters, was this done, when a German physicist, Heinrich Hertz, showed that it was possible. Working at the Technical College at Karlsruhe, he developed an apparatus which was in two parts. The first part, which we should now call the transmitter, consisted of two brass balls set half an inch apart. A spark was caused to jump across this space by applying a high electrical potential to the balls.

A few feet away he erected a two-and-a-half foot diameter ring of wire, broken at one point by a narrow gap. Although this ring was not connected in any way with the brass balls, he noticed that when a spark jumped the space between the balls, a spark appeared simultaneously across the break in the wire. He concluded that energy had been transferred across the intervening space by the electromagnetic waves described by Clerk Maxwell. He studied these waves, and found, as Maxwell had predicted, that they were similar to light waves, but of different wavelength.

Although he published the results of his experiments, he treated them simply as interesting phenomena, and made no suggestions as to any practical uses to which they might be put. But inevitably others, who read his publication, thought along those lines.

In 1892 Sir William Crookes, writing in the *Fortnightly Review*, suggested that electromagnetic waves or 'Hertzian' waves, as they were now called, should be used for sending messages through space. The suggestion attracted the attention of another physicist, Sir Oliver Lodge, of the University of Birmingham, who began to experiment with a communication system using Hertzian waves.

His transmitter was a development of Hertz's apparatus, using two similar brass balls, but his receiver was much improved. It had an aerial, a tuned circuit, a detector consisting of a device called a 'coherer' which had been invented by Edouard Branly in Paris in 1890, and a relay which controlled an electro-magnetic telegraph recorder. It contained, in fact, all the essentials of a practical wireless telegraph receiver. This apparatus he called a 'cymoscope' from the Greek word for a wave. By means of it he succeeded, by 1894, in sending Morse code messages over a distance of half a mile. Other inventors working along similar lines were Ernest Rutherford, Lee Forest in America, and in Italy Guglielmo Marconi.

The most successful of these was Marconi. Unlike the inventor of popular fiction he was not born in poverty, selling newspapers to buy equipment and burning the midnight oil after a hard day's work. His father was a successful business man of Bologna where Marconi was born on April 25th, 1874. He was educated by a private tutor and his main interests were music and electrical science. He was an accomplished pianist, and read widely on the subject of electricity. His mother, who was Irish, encouraged him in both these pursuits, and helped him to set up his own laboratory at home, persuading his father to find the necessary money. Here he spent much of his time studying and experimenting with electricity, but not in any particular aspect of the subject. One year, whilst staying at Leghorn with his family he met an old blind telegrapher, from whom he learnt the Morse code. In spite of this, however, his thoughts did not turn to telegraphy, and he continued his electrical experiments without any particular aim in mind.

Early in 1894, a few weeks before his twentieth birthday, Marconi went for a holiday in the Alps with his step-brother Luigi. While on holiday he came across a periodical in which there was an article on the work of Heinrich Hertz, who had died a few months before. It described his work on electromagnetic waves.

Marconi, though he knew there was already a theory about the possible existence of such waves, was not aware until he read this article that their existence had actually been proved. He immediately saw the use to which this phenomenon could be put. In his own words: 'I conceived the idea that by means of the invention of efficient telegraphic transmitters and receivers it would be possible to transmit and receive messages over great distances without the necessity of using connecting wires.' His aim was clear; from then on he set to work to produce a practical means of communication using the phenomenon of electromagnetic waves. In this he was so successful that, though only an enthusiastic amateur, he soon outstripped the professional scientists and engineers.

After a year's work he had developed apparatus which would transmit messages up to 300 yards. He approached the Italian Government to see if they would be interested in this new form of communication. They were not, and so he decided to go to England where his mother had many influential relatives and friends. In February 1896 he and his mother arrived in London and took a house in Westbourne Park, Bayswater. His first action was to patent his invention and this was done on June 2nd, 1896—the first patent in the world to be granted for wireless telegraphy.

One of his introductions was to Mr. William (later Sir William) Preece, Chief Engineer of the General Post Office. Mr. Preece was immediately impressed by Marconi's invention and arranged for his engineers to conduct a test. This took place on the roof of the Post Office at St. Martin's-le-Grand, and messages were successfully sent to another building a quarter of a mile away.

As a result of this test, and the backing he received from Mr. Preece, Marconi was asked to give demonstrations to senior officers of the Army and Royal Navy. His invention had obvious military applications.

These demonstrations took place on Salisbury Plain, in the late summer of 1896, and this time he succeeded in establishing a system of communications over two miles. The War Office was anxious to take the invention up, and Marconi's success was assured.

The apparatus used by Marconi was in principle the same as that which Sir Oliver Lodge had developed two years before, but with several improvements, the principal one being the use of an earth at transmitter and receiver. The former consisted of two pairs of metal balls between which a continuous series of electric sparks was produced by applying a high-voltage current from an induction coil. By means of a Morse key in the primary circuit of the induction coil the sparking could be interrupted as required to produce signals in the Morse Code.

The balls were connected to an aerial circuit, of a certain fixed inductance, one end of which was earthed, and the other connected to the aerial, a length of wire about 100 feet long, suspended from a balloon or kite. Each spark set up oscillations of current at a high frequency in the aerial circuit and caused electromagnetic (or 'wireless') waves to be radiated from the aerial. The whole apparatus was known as a spark transmitter.

The receiver had a similar aerial and earth and an aerial circuit 'tuned' to the same frequency as the transmitter by matching its inductance. Thus the electromagnetic waves radiated by the aerial of the transmitter were picked up in the receiver. They were still high-frequency oscillations, and could not be detected by any of the usual telegraph instruments, so some form of detector was required. This took the form of a 'coherer', a small horizontal glass tube containing loose metal filings (Marconi used filings of tin). Each end was connected to the aerial circuit, and when the high-frequency

THE FIRST TRANSATLANTIC MESSAGE

oscillations passed through the coherer they had the effect of making the metal filings cohere, or join together. In this state they formed an electrical conductor and allowed a low-voltage, direct current to flow in a secondary circuit where it produced a signal in a telephone headset, or operated, through a relay, a magnetic recording instrument.

After each signal the coherer had to be tapped, to loosen the filings in preparation for the next signal. In Marconi's early sets this was done by hand, which restricted the speed of transmission, but he soon fitted an automatic device to do it. This consisted of an armature and tapper like those of an electric bell, which was operated by the signal itself through the secondary circuit.

Following his early demonstrations Marconi decided the way was now open for the expansion and development of his system. He formed a company to manufacture and operate wireless equipment. It was called the Wireless Telegraph and Signal Company (later changed to the Marconi Wireless Telegraph Company), with laboratories and workshops at Chelmsford. Marconi left the business side of the Company to others and continued to carry on with research. To help him he secured the services not only of able business men, but also of highly qualified scientists. The most famous of these was Professor Sir James Ambrose Fleming of University College, London, who held the post of scientific adviser to the Marconi Company. A great inventor in his own right, he was later to revolutionise wireless telegraphy, and make possible wireless telephony, by the invention of the thermionic valve.

Marconi, however, remained the driving force behind the work of the company, although only 24 years of age. He was a man of tremendous energy and when tackling a particular problem he would not spare himself, and thought nothing of going two or three nights without sleep. He expected a similar dedication from those who worked with him.

He would never disclose information about any new development until absolutely certain that he had accomplished what he had set out to do. He knew the value of publicity, however, and as soon as he had accomplished anything likely to interest the general public he saw that the press received information of it in such a way as to catch the public imagination. Thus, in 1898 he set up a wireless transmitter in a small steamship, the *Flying Huntress*, and used her to follow the yachts taking part in the Kingstown Regatta. A running comment on the races was transmitted to a station on shore, telephoned to the offices of the *Dublin Express*, and printed in special editions so that readers could follow the races while the yachts were still at sea. Without a doubt this must have been the first wireless sports commentary in the world, and it caused a sensation. It came to the attention of Queen Victoria, who requested Marconi to establish wireless communication between her and the Prince of Wales during Cowes week. A station was set up in the grounds of Osborne House, in the Isle of Wight, where the Queen was in residence, and on board the royal yacht where the Prince of Wales was spending regatta week. The Queen was able to keep in touch and receive regular bulletins from the doctor in attendance on the Prince, who was suffering from an injured leg. Again Marconi's work came into the public view.

As well as the first sports commentary, Marconi may fairly be credited with being the first to fit a wireless receiver to a road vehicle. In 1901 a steam-propelled waggonette was fitted with a tubular-shaped aerial on its roof and a receiver inside. True, it was really a mobile station and not intended to be used for receiving messages while in motion, but it was none the less the forerunner of the car-radio of today.

Another valuable source of publicity to Marconi was a permanent station which he set up in the grounds of the Needles Hotel in the Isle of Wight. From here he communicated with his other station at Poole, on the mainland. The Needles station was opened to the public, who could watch this modern marvel at work, just as nearly seventy years before the public had flocked to Paddington station to pay a shilling in order to watch Cooke and Wheatstone's first electric telegraph at work.

Unlike a modern wireless transmitter, Marconi's apparatus did have something really impressive to show to the Isle of Wight holiday-makers who came to see it at work. As the young men who operated the transmitter tapped at their Morse keys, the electric sparks crashed out again and again across the spark gap, suggesting to the onlooker vast and mysterious forces harnessed to man's use. It was exciting as well as mysterious.

The following March Marconi received some unsought publicity when a cargo ship the *R. F. Matthews* collided with the East Goodwin

Lightship. The Marconi Company had fitted the lightship with a wireless link to the Dungeness Lighthouse, and help was quickly summoned by a distress signal from the transmitter on board.

In 1897 Marconi communicated across the Bristol Channel from Lavernock Point in South Wales to Brean Down in Somerset. The English Channel was the next obstacle to be tackled and he set up a station at Wimereux for cross-channel tests. On Monday, March 27th, 1899, he made the first successful cross-channel communication with the station at Poole.

The opening of the twentieth century found Marconi and his wireless system well established in the world of communications. The value of the system had been proved without any doubt, especially in its use by vessels at sea, this being the field which Marconi's company had set out to exploit. Now he turned his thoughts to widening the scope of his experiments and using wireless as a means of long-distance communication.

His thoughts turned to the Atlantic, as had those of others before him, and as would those of others still to come. The conquest of the Atlantic, the joining of the Old World with the New seems to be an inevitable step in the development of new communications—steamships, telegraphs, wireless, and later the air. It marks the threshold between experiment and practice; the point from which commercial development can proceed; the stage which impresses the new development on the consciousness of the public. Marconi decided that the time had come to transmit by wireless across the Atlantic.

Now came a test of his personality. He had to persuade the directors of the company to spend £50,000 on an experiment which many leading scientists described as impossible. Scientific objections were raised, as they were when an Atlantic cable was proposed. But this time they seemed to be based on more solid ground. How, said the critics, could wireless waves possibly be sent round the curved surface of the world if they behaved in the same manner as light, and therefore travelled in straight lines? No light, however powerful, could be projected across the Atlantic, and so it followed that wireless waves could not be sent either. So ran the argument; and it seemed sound.

Marconi did not try to argue scientifically against this theory. He was not a scientist, but only an enthusiastic amateur. He relied to a large extent on his scientific advisers. But he had a hunch that long-distance communication was possible. He had already communicated with ships at sea long after they had disappeared below the horizon. He was convinced that transmitting across the Atlantic was feasible, and his fellow directors were persuaded. In 1901 work began on the project.

The original plan was to have two stations each transmitting and receiving. One was to be at Poldhu in Cornwall, and the other at Cape Cod, Massachusetts. At each of these places a giant aerial installation was erected, consisting of twenty wooden masts each 200 feet high. These were arranged in a circle 200 feet in diameter, and between them was strung a network of wires. To the astonished inhabitants of Poldhu, watching the aerial array as it grew it must have seemed like some modernistic, electric, Stonehenge. The Druids had returned to Cornwall in the form of Marconi and his technicians! But their magic was to prove greater than anything the ancient Druids could have imagined.

The transmitter, which was built to the design of Professor Fleming, and of which he was in charge, was of the familiar spark type; but like the aerial it was built to a much greater scale than any before it. Its wavelength is not known, for at that time no means of calibrating the apparatus existed. But Professor Fleming, in later years, calculated that it must have been about 960 metres. Power, which was ten times that of any previous transmitter, was supplied, not by cells, but by an alternator driven by a 25 horse-power oil engine.

By the end of August 1901 all was ready for the experiment to begin. The giant aerial array, which covered the best part of an acre, was connected up to the transmitter. Then on September 17th a violent gale blew up, and in one night the whole of the aerial system was demolished. Worse still, a few days later that at Cape Cod was wrecked in the same way.

To rebuild both systems would take some months, and Marconi was anxious to get on with his experiments. He altered his plans, and instead of two-way communication across the Atlantic he decided that he would now have to make do with a one-way link.

He decided that his transmitter would be at Poldhu, where Fleming could remain in charge of it, and he set to work immediately to build a new aerial system. This time he used only two masts, each 150 feet high, and 180 feet apart. At the top they were joined by a stay, from which were suspended 55 copper wires forming a fan shape—a yard apart at the top and joined together at the bottom. The power transmitted from this aerial would be less than that from his original one, while the signals would have to be received on a smaller and less sensitive aerial. To overcome this difficulty it was essential that the distance between transmitter and receiver should not be too great. He could, of course, have got over this difficulty by transmitting to a ship at sea, somewhere out in the Atlantic ocean. But Marconi knew the value of publicity; he wanted the prestige of a transtlantic communication from the Old World to the New. He looked at the map and chose the only place he could for his experiment—Newfoundland. The closest point to Europe, it was some thousand miles nearer than Cape Cod. No time was lost, and at the end of November Marconi and his assistants were on the S.S. *Sardinian* bound from Liverpool to St. John's.

They were a small party. Besides Marconi there were his two assistants, Mr. G. S. Kemp and Mr. P. W. Paget. Kemp had been Marconi's right-hand man ever since his first arrival in England. Down below in the ship's hold were several hampers containing the wireless equipment and several kites and balloons to take aloft the temporary aerials they would be using. Twenty-five cylinders of hydrogen gas for the balloons completed the cargo. Apart from these things, they entered the New World as ordinary travellers, and their arrival in St. John's went almost unnoticed.

They put up at the Cochrane Hotel in Cochrane Street, at that time the principal hotel in St. John's. Here the young Italian inventor was interviewed by the reporter of the city's *Evening Telegram*, who referred to him in Churchillian style as 'Mr. William Marconi'. He had come, he told the reporter, as a result of correspondence he had had with Mr. Murphy, the Newfoundland Minister of Marine and Fisheries. Mr. Murphy had written to him about the large number of shipwrecks that took place along the coast of Newfoundland, and about the possibility of setting up a wireless telegraph station in the island to warn shipping of dangers. His object was to carry out experiments for this purpose.

He made no mention at all of the real object of his visit. That was not Marconi's way. All his life he preferred to do his preliminary work in secret. Not until he had successfully completed that which he had set out to do did he release news of it to the world, and then only when he was absolutely sure of his success. Nowhere was this more apparent than in his transatlantic project.

On December 7th, the day after his arrival, Marconi called on the Governor, Sir Cavendish Boyle, and the Prime Minister, Sir Robert Bond. Both these gentlemen showed a lively interest in his experiments and offered him any help that the Colony's resources could provide.

The same day Marconi and his assistants, with Mr. Murphy, the Minister of Marine, and Mr. White, Inspector of Lighthouses, set out to find a suitable site for a wireless station. They had not far to look. Signal Hill, standing guard over the Narrows and facing out across the Atlantic, was the obvious choice. Even its name was prophetic!

On the plateau at the top of the hill was the old fever hospital, formerly a naval barracks. Marconi decided to make the western end of this his depot for the tests, and it was arranged that a local contractor, Mr. Moore, should cart the apparatus up to it and in addition would cover the ground around it with large sheets of zinc to form an 'earth'. By the efforts of Mr. Murphy a room in the ground floor of the Cabot Tower was put at the disposal of the inventor.

This is how Marconi himself described his choice:

'After taking a look at various sites which might prove suitable, I considered the best one on Signal Hill, a lofty eminence overlooking the port and forming a natural bulwark which protects it from the fury of the Atlantic winds. On top of the hill is a small plateau some two acres in extent which seemed very suitable for the manipulation of the balloons and kites. On a crag on this plateau rose the new Cabot Tower, erected in commemoration of the famous Italian explorer John Cabot and designed as a signal station. Close to it was the old military barracks, then used as a hospital. It was in the forum of this building that we set up the apparatus and made preparations for the great experiment.

'On Monday December 9th we began work. On Tuesday we flew a kite with 600 feet of aerial as a preliminary test, and on Wednesday we inflated one of the balloons which made its first ascent in the morning. It was about 14 feet in diameter and contained about 1000 cubic feet of hydrogen gas, quite sufficient to hold up the aerial which consisted of a wire weighing about ten pounds. After a short while however the blustery wind ripped the balloon away from the wire. The balloon sailed out over the sea. We concluded, perhaps the kites would be better, and on Thursday morning in spite of a gusty gale we managed to fly a kite up to 400 feet.

'The critical moment had come, for which the way had been prepared by six years of hard and unremitting work, despite the usual criticisms levelled at anything new. I was about to test the truth of my belief.

'In view of the importance of all that was at stake, I decided not to trust entirely to the usual arrangement of having the coherer signals record automatically on a paper tape through a relay and Morse instrument, but to use instead a telephone connected to a self-restoring coherer. The human ear being much more sensitive than the recorder, it would be more likely to hear the signal.

'Before leaving England I had given detailed instructions for transmission of a certain signal, the Morse telegraphic "S"—three dots—at a fixed time each day beginning as soon as word was received that everything at St. John's was in readiness. If the invention would receive on the kite-wire in Newfoundland, some of the electric waves produced, I knew that the solution of the problem of transoceanic wireless telegraphy was at hand.

'I cabled Poldhu to begin sending (on December 12th) at 3 p.m. in the afternoon English time, continuing until 6 o'clock, that is from 11.30 a.m. to 2.30 p.m. at St. John's.'

As already mentioned, on the morning of Thursday, December 12th, a kite carrying the aerial had been successfully flown to a height of 400 feet. The end of the aerial led in through one of the windows of the bottom floor of the Cabot Tower, where the receiving apparatus had been set up. While upstairs the look-out on duty scanned the sea through his telescope, watching for signals from ships two or three miles out in the Atlantic, Marconi and his two assistants down below scanned the ether, waiting for signals from Poldhu, in England, two thousand miles away, on the other side of the same ocean. The atmosphere was tense as Marconi sat listening and straining his ears. Here is how he described what happened.

'Suddenly at about 12.30 p.m. unmistakably three scant little clicks in the telephone receiver sounded several times in my ears, as I listened intently. But I would not be satisfied without corroboration. 'Can you hear anything, Kemp?' I said, handing him the receiver. Kemp heard the same thing that I did, and I knew then that I was absolutely right in my anticipation. Electric waves which had been sent out from Poldhu had traversed the Atlantic, serenely ignoring the curvature of the earth which so many doubters considered would be a fatal obstacle. I knew then that the day would come on which I should be able to send full messages without wires or cables across the Atlantic was not very far away. Distance had been overcome, and further developments of the sending and receiving apparatus were all that was required.'

Again and again as they listened they heard the three dots repeated. They called in Paget, who had been outside, keeping his eye on the kite. But he was slightly deaf, and could not hear the signals. About 2 oclock the kite dropped, and the signals disappeared. But at 2.20 the wind freshened, the kite rose again, and the signals came through once more, loud and clear until the transmissions ceased at 2.30. There was no doubt that they had received signals from Poldhu—there was no other station in the world from which they might have come.

They wound in the kite, put away their apparatus, and walked slowly down Signal Hill to the town. Marconi might have been excused if, like John Bowring, he had dashed down the hill, full of excitement, to cable his momentous news to the world and the press. But that was not his way. He always waited until he was absolutely certain.

Unlike the submarine telegraph, the successful bridging of the Atlantic by wireless telegraphy remained unknown to the world for two days. During that time Marconi and his assistants kept the secret to themselves. Finally, after another day of successful reception, on Saturday, December 14th, Marconi released his news to the press. On Sunday, December 15th, the papers first carried news that wireless signals had been successfully transmitted across the Atlantic. There was a rush of newspaper reporters towards St. John's. But Marconi realised the necessity of proving without a shadow of doubt that his attempt had succeeded, and so on the following Tuesday he invited a party of notable people in St. John's to witness a demonstration. The Governor, Sir Cavendish Boyle, and the Prime Minister of Newfoundland Sir Robert Bond were members of the party that assembled that day in the Cabot Tower to hear for themselves the Morse signals flashed from the transmitter at Poldhu. Also in the party were Sir Frederick and Sir Edgar Bowring, sons of old John Bowring who forty years ago had stood on Signal Hill watching the returning sealing fleet. Their minds must have gone back to an August day in 1866 when, as small boys, they had stood on the deck of the Bowring steamer *Hawk* off Heart's Content, listening to the thunder of *Great Eastern*'s paddles beating the calm waters of Trinity Bay into foam as they went astern and the great ship hove to at the end of her successful laying of the Atlantic cable. Now they were witnessing another great leap forward in the development of communications, a change that looked as though it might make the submarine cable obsolete.

The news of Marconi's success created a sensation all over the world, though in America the great inventor Thomas Edison refused to believe it and even went so far as to suggest that it was a 'newspaper fake'. In Newfoundland the reporter of the *Evening Telegram* paid another visit to the Cochrane Hotel, and in the ensuing report, bristling with superlatives and arresting sub-titles, paid his tribute to the modest inventor.

'Wireless telegraphy at long distances', he reported, 'is an accomplished fact, for Marconi has spoken to a man 1,900 miles away, with no other medium than that which existed on the morning that Noah came out of the Ark. Nature grudgingly gave out
THE GREAT SECRET
but, bit by bit, Marconi made the bold venture and subdued the hidden secrets of Dame Nature to obey his own will. The very thought of it sets one aghast. The humble genius who received the Telegram reporter at the Cochrane Hotel makes no vain-glorious boast about what he has achieved. He is as modest as a schoolboy and one would not think that he is the wizard who wrought this awe-inspiring wonder of science, that realizes the tales of the Arabian Nights and the stories of Jules Verne. It is no wonder that New York stood astounded and refused to believe the news when it was flashed over the wires on Saturday night. Newspapers were sceptical and before sending the report to their printers wired for

CONFIRMATION OF THE NEWS

The citizens of St. John's even doubted the truth of it on Saturday night. They had cast an occasional glance up at Signal Hill the past few days while the experiments were going on. They had seen electrically-charged kites whirling in the storm-tossed air over Signal Hill, but did not attach much importance to the matter. . . .

NOWISE THE LESS

Wednesday the 11th December, 1901, will be put down as a memorable day in the history of the world—a day on which one of the greatest achievements in science was accomplished. It will be a proud boast for the people of Newfoundland to say in the words of the poet, when looking back on it, "magna pars quorum fuimus". We heartily congratulate Signor Marconi on his success! There is a fascination in imagining him sitting at his table in the building on Signal Hill, with watch in hand, waiting for the hand to point to the moment agreed upon with his friend on the other side of the Atlantic. The hand moves slowly around, the scientist's mind is

STRUNG TO POWERFUL TENSION.

Will the dreams of his life—of his soul's ambition—be realized? A quiver like an angel's breath breathes over the receiving instruments, and the delicate recorder begins to move, low as the whisper of a dying child at first, but in half a minute gaining strength. The secret of the age was being yielded grudgingly, as it were, to the listening ear of the High Priest of electoral [sic] science—Signor Marconi. The sounds were now distinct, and what ravishing music they made when the three dots of the letter S (. . . . .) were repeated

GROWING STRONGER EACH TIME.

A new spirit was born to science with a tip of its wing on each side of the ocean. The old Atlantic cable heard the news, quivered and groaned. Telegraph cable stocks slumped on the market on Saturday evening, and there was fever-heat excitement among business men.'

The next day Marconi was the guest of honour at a public luncheon at Government House, St. John's, the first of many such occasions on both sides of the Atlantic. When the speeches and congratulations were over Marconi departed for Cape Spear, a few miles south of St. John's. Here, with Newfoundland officials, he reconnoitred a site for a permanent wireless station. As soon as possible he wished to experiment with his wireless to see if it could be used commercially.

His plans were interrupted, and his association with Newfoundland was abruptly cut short, however, for when he returned he found waiting for him at the Cochrane Hotel a solicitor acting on behalf of the Anglo-American Telegraph Company, who handed him a letter which threatened a court injunction restraining him from receiving any more telegraph messages from outside Newfoundland. By the terms of their Act of 1854, which still had three years to run, the company had the sole right to land telegraph cables and receive telegraph messages in Newfoundland for fifty years. They intended to enforce it in the Newfoundland courts.

It was hardly surprising that the cable company was worried. With the success of Marconi's experiments, newspapers and journals had been quick to point out the obvious economy of the new system of communication compared with submarine telegraphs. Its limitations were not yet realised, and it appeared to be a formidable competitor to the cable. Whereas the first Atlantic cable had cost £2,765,000 and the labour of hundreds of men, Marconi had achieved his result with an outlay of only £50,000, and, as far as the receiving end at Newfoundland was concerned, with the work of only himself and two other men. The contrast was too obvious to be overlooked, and at the time no one could foresee that the rapid increase in the volume of world communication together with the extra reliability of cables would make the two systems complementary to each other. The immediate reaction of the public to the news of Marconi's success was reflected in a sharp drop in the price of Anglo-American shares on the stock exchanges.

Nor was it only the Anglo-American Company that was alarmed. Mr. Ward, President of their rivals, the Commercial Cable Company, when interviewd by the press, indulged in a little wishful thinking and stated as his opinion the belief that Signor Marconi had mistaken for signals the action of the ground current or that of lightning, explaining that his company frequently got letters of the alphabet over the cable in this way.

The only effect of the cable company's action on Marconi was to cause him to sever his connection with Newfoundland. As soon as the news of the prohibition was published he was overwhelmed with offers of sites for his station in Canada and U.S.A. Professor

Graham Bell, the inventor of the telephone, offered his estate near Buddeck, Nova Scotia. The Canadian Government also offered him facilities, and he still had his station at Cape Cod. He accordingly abandoned his idea for a station at Cape Spear, or anywhere else in Newfoundland, and, not without reluctance, left the country from whose representatives he had received the greatest hospitality.

There was considerable indignation in St. John's at the action of the company, and a feeling that Newfoundland had been cheated of her rightful part in this new world-wide development. Our old acquaintance Mr. A. M. Mackay, still Superintendent of the Anglo-American Company in Newfoundland, came in for much criticism. He replied through the press that he was as desirous as any man to help in the cause of scientific progress in wireless telegraphy, but pointed out that, being the responsible representative of the Anglo-American Company, he would be recreant to his duty if he did not look to the interests of the company and safeguard its rights.

Marconi left St. John's on December 22nd, departing by the 5 p.m. train for Port-aux-Basques on his way to Nova Scotia. Never in all its history had the little railway station at Fort William seen such a send-off as this. By this time newspaper reporters from all over America and Europe had arrived in St. John's and they were at the station to see him off. They reported that fishermen and farmers with their families from miles around had gathered to get a glimpse of this quiet, unassuming man of 27 who had made history on that December day in the first year of the twentieth century. The train pulled out to the cheers and waves of the crowd.

Thus ended Marconi's brief connection with Newfoundland. He had been in the country only fourteen days, but the results of that fortnight had, quite literally, electrified the world. Wireless telegraphy had arrived.

Today, Signal Hill is a National Park, and the Cabot Tower a National Monument. Close beside it is an obelisk of granite, on which is recorded for posterity the story of that day in December 1901 when the Old World and the New were linked for the first time by wireless waves.

PART FOUR
CONQUEST OF THE ATLANTIC BY AIR

CHAPTER 8

The Daily Mail *Prize—First Attempts*

IN THE SCIENCE MUSEUM at South Kensington, London, there is a department devoted to historic aircraft. They hang suspended from a lofty ceiling as though suddenly immobilised while in flight. A spiral staircase leading to a catwalk enables visitors to walk among them, to peer into cockpits that remind one of an open sports car, and to marvel at the fragility of the early flying machines.

The largest of them is a Vickers *Vimy* bomber of the first world war. The notice describing it reads as follows:

'VICKERS VIMY, 1919

'This was the first aircraft to make a direct non-stop flight across the Atlantic. The flight was made by Alcock and Brown on 14th and 15th June 1919 from St. John's, Newfoundland, to Clifden, Co. Galway, Ireland. The distance from coast to coast of 1,880 miles was covered in 15 hours, 57 minutes at an average speed of 118·5 miles per hour.'

Behind this brief description lies a story not just of two men, but of many—a story of adventure, heroism, endurance and self-sacrifice; the story of a challenge and the way in which it was met.

The challenge was the linking of the Old World and the New by air, and to begin the story we must go as far back as 1910.

On October 15th of that year an American aviator, Walter Wellman, set out to achieve what critics almost unanimously declared to be impossible—to fly the Atlantic in his dirigible airship *America*.

At this time in the history of aviation the airship or lighter-than-air machine still had a supremacy over the aeroplane, or heavier-than-air flying machine. It was only seven years since the Wright brothers had made their first tentative hop of twelve seconds off the ground; only a year since Louis Bleriot had just managed to coax his monoplane over the English Channel. Airships, on the other hand, had flown distances of up to 600 miles non-stop and could carry much heavier loads than the aeroplane. The Atlantic, however, even at its narrowest point, was nearly 2,000 miles; hence the disbelief of the critics. Their attitude was excusable, to some extent, for on a previous occasion Wellman had announced a plan to fly over the North Pole to Spitzbergen, but had never carried out his intention.

It was not surprising, therefore, that on the morning of October 15th there was only his wife, with a few friends, to see him off from his mooring ground at Atlantic City.

The *America* was an airship of semi-rigid type; that is, she had a 'keel' which ran almost the whole length of the aircraft and to which the engines, gondola, and rudder and elevators were attached. The envelope was not, however, contained in a rigid framework, as was done with later and larger airships, such as the Zeppelins. She was 230 feet long with a diameter of 50 feet at the widest point, and was powered by two 90 horse-power petrol motors, each driving two airscrews. Total weight of the machine was twelve and a half tons.

For this particular flight the *America* had received several additions to her usual equipment. This was before the days of inflatable rubber dinghies, so in case of forced descent the airship carried an ordinary ship's lifeboat slung beneath the gondola. A quick-release mechanism similar to that used by naval vessels allowed the boat to be dropped into the water from a height of a few feet. In due course the crew were to be extremely thankful for this equipment, but while flying its weight and air resistance must have been a considerable drawback.

A wireless set was also carried to enable them to keep in touch with the world during the four or five days which they expected to take for the trip; and lastly a drogue was fitted in the form of a long canvas tube which trailed in the water below them. This contained petrol for the motors; in this way they hoped to take part of the weight of the fuel in the sea during the early stages of the journey.

In addition to Wellman there was a crew of five, of various nationalities. Three of them were mechanics, one a navigator and one a wireless operator. A black cat completed the airship's complement.

The ropes were cast off and the airship moved out to sea, towed by a tug. As soon as she was well off shore the towline was cast off, and at a height of about 100 feet the *America* moved slowly out of sight.

Wellman's plan was to fly along the Atlantic seaboard, keeping within sight of land, past Cape Breton and up the west coast of Newfoundland to the straits of Belle Isle, then eastwards across the Atlantic for Europe. In this way he was able to keep close to land until the last possible moment, but against this had to be weighed the fact that they were moving at a height of only 100 feet in waters frequented by shipping, with the drogue dragging behind them in the sea. It is difficult to understand why Wellman did not instead fly to Newfoundland, refuel there, and start out on the last leg of the journey with his crew fresh.

Throughout the day of October 15th the *America* made her way north-east. By 20.00 hours she was somewhere off Long Island, still flying at 100 feet, and with visibility reduced by the falling dusk and a sea-mist. Suddenly the mist cleared, and a few feet ahead of the airship was a four-masted sailing ship. She was the barque *Bullard* out of Boston and bound for Norfolk, Virginia. Wellman, who was at the controls, just had time to alter course and the two vessels, airship and sailing ship, passed so close to each other that the crew of the barque were able to feel the heat of the airship's exhaust.

From this moment trouble of one kind or another dogged them. One of the engines seized up and they flew throughout the night on one engine. The wireless transmitter would not work, and the signals received were faint. The *America* was gradually losing what little height she had, and dawn revealed them to be off Nantucket Island—not very far on their way. The reasonable thing would have been to give up the attempt and turn back. But Wellman probably felt that he could not risk another fiasco, so he kept the airship's nose north-eastwards and they flew on over the Atlantic Ocean.

During the day wireless stations all along the eastern seaboard tried to contact the *America*. It was urgent that they should warn her of a violent hurricane which had swept over Cuba and was now heading north across the course of the airship; but there was no reply to their calls. In fact, the *America* was some 200 miles out in the Atlantic Ocean, being carried off course by a strong north-westerly wind. They could now no longer turn back, as with their single engine they had insufficient power to make any headway against the wind. By evening Wellman realised that there was only one thing he could do. He turned south-east and ran before the wind, hoping to reach Bermuda.

They were still drifting lower, and to lighten the airship they dropped the seized engine. The drogue went also and all the fuel not needed to reach Bermuda. All through the night and the following day they battled on. They were off the main sea routes now, and there was no sign of shipping. The night came again and the single remaining engine began to give trouble. Their hopes of reaching land started to fade.

At half-past four, in the darkness just before the dawn, they saw the lights of a ship. Irwin, the wireless operator, seized the key of the transmitter and sent out the C.Q.D. call—the distress signal. He listened anxiously for a reply, and after a few agonising moments delay it came through. The ship was in range of his transmitter.

The vessel was the S.S. *Trent*, outward bound from Bermuda, and she prepared to take the airship's crew on board. It was too dark to attempt a rescue yet, so the *Trent* turned and steamed in the direction of the drifting gasbag. After two hours it was light enough to launch the airship's lifeboat. The crew took their places in it while Wellman opened the gas valves and brought the *America* down to a few feet from the surface of the water. He took his place in the boat, the release mechanism was pulled, and the boat dropped into the water. Relieved of its weight the airship lifted slightly and blew away over the sea.

The crew of the *America* rowed alongside the *Trent* and were taken on board all safe and sound, including the cat. So ended the first attempt to fly the Atlantic, a failure, but a gallant one. They had covered 1,008 miles.

Two years later Melville Vaniman, who had been one of Wellman's crew in the *America*, made the second attempt in an airship of his own design, the *Akron*, the first of the two vessels that carried that ill-fated name. On July 2nd, 1912, the *Akron* left Atlantic City on its third test flight, and fifteen minutes later suddenly burst into flames and was lost with all its five crew. Like all early airships it suffered from the grave disadvantage of employing hydrogen gas as a lifting agent, and hydrogen is highly inflammable.

By this time progress in the design of the heavier-than-air machine was catching up with the airship. In Britain encouragement came from the *Daily Mail*, the national newspaper owned by Lord Northcliffe. Concerned at the lack of interest shown by the British Government in the development of aviation, compared with the efforts of other countries, Lord Northcliffe, through the *Daily Mail*, made the following outstanding offer. It appeared in that paper on April 1st, 1913 (a curious date to choose for a serious offer!).

VAST DAILY MAIL PRIZES
The Air Problem
The Waterplane, Britain's Best Weapon.
£5,000 – Circuit of England and Scotland.
£10,000 – Flight across Atlantic.
Aeroplane? Waterplane? or Airship?

We offer £10,000 to the first person who crosses the Atlantic from any point in the United States, Canada, or Newfoundland, to any point in Great Britain or Ireland in 72 continuous hours. The flight may be made, of course, either way across the Atlantic. The prize is open to pilots of any nationality and machines of foreign as well as British construction.

New developments are coming so thick and fast that Great Britain has not a moment to lose. We want to see less national supineness and far more energetic action in this all important matter of air defence. That the British Government should remain inert and apathetic while other powers are busy night and day in the construction of engines of war which may be used against ourselves is not in accordance with the traditions of enterprise, determination and foresight that have made the British Empire what it is.

The *Daily Mail* offer aroused tremendous interest in aviation circles. Flying was still very much a sport indulged in by enthusiasts; it was carried on in the spirit which still survives today in the world of motor racing, 'scrambles', and rallies, but it also had the appeal of a pioneer activity which was constantly exploring new grounds. The early fliers were still few in numbers, and known to each other as fellow-members of a brotherhood; most of them had learnt to fly the hard way by trial and error, in crazy 'string-bags' with tiny engines. They were members of a select band flying planes most of which were 'one off' jobs. The war, with its mass-production of planes and also of aviators, was to change all that, but for the moment it was this small band of airmen who received the offer of the *Daily Mail* with enthusiasm.

Many of them set to work making plans to take on the challenge. Gustave Hamel, one of the best-known British pilots, was able to obtain private backing, from Mr. McKay Edgar, a wealthy Canadian Scot, and no doubt to the envy of many others he immediately commissioned the Martinsyde Company of Woking, Surrey, to build a special plane for the flight. It was designed as a monoplane, with an undercarriage that could be detached and dropped after take off, thus reducing air resistance and weight. It also had buoyancy tanks fitted, in case it came down in the sea, and a telescopic mast so that passing vessels could be signalled.

This aeroplane was to be ready for an attempt in the summer of 1914, but unfortunately, when it was three-quarters completed, the death of Hamel in an air crash in the Channel put an end, for the time being, to the project.

The challenge was also taken up in America, where Mr. Rodman Wanamaker, a New York millionaire store owner, commissioned a flying boat from the Curtiss Aircraft Company. He chose a British pilot to fly it, a Lieutenant Porte. The plane was ready by June 1914, and on its test flights all went well. Before taking off for Newfoundland, where the transatlantic flight would begin, Lieut. Porte gave it a full scale test, carrying the load of fuel it would need to cross the Atlantic. To his mortification, all the skill he possessed was insufficient to get the plane into the air. The two 100 horse-power motors just could not provide enough thrust. The attempt had to be abandoned, and before more powerful motors could be fitted war had broken out, and the attack on the Atlantic had to be postponed.

In England, all civil flying was prohibited on the outbreak of war in August 1914. The *Daily Mail* also withdrew their offer of £10,000, and aviators had other and less pleasant matters to occupy them. So for the next five years the Atlantic remained unconquered. But during this time, under the stimulus of war, the design of aircraft made tremendous progress, and by 1918 there were several long-distance bombers, able to fly to Berlin and back. It was obvious that as soon as conditions permitted an attempt could be made on the Atlantic crossing. Many airmen laid their plans throughout the dark days of the war, and before the conflict had ended the *Daily Mail* had renewed its offer. On July 17th, 1918, the newspaper announced that in order to stimulate the production of more powerful engines and more suitable aircraft, the prize of £10,000 for an Atlantic crossing would again be offered on the same terms.

The Armistice came in November 1918 and almost immediately a number of projects were put in hand to make an attempt on the crossing the following summer. Almost every aircraft firm in Britain had plans for a transatlantic winner, for they all realised the enormous publicity value attached to a successful attempt. About a dozen projects were put in hand, and in every case but one they planned to fly the Atlantic from west to east, for in that direction the prevailing winds would assist the aircraft. They naturally chose the shortest route, and so the obvious place to start from was Newfoundland.

Thus it came about that in the spring of 1919 St. John's was subject to an invasion, albeit a friendly one, of aviators with their machines, all bent on winning the *Daily Mail* £10,000 prize. It was peculiarly appropriate that the attempt should start from Newfoundland, for the printing presses of the *Daily Mail* and its associated publications were fed with newsprint that came from Grand Falls in the north of the island, where in 1910 Lord Northcliffe had formally opened the paper mills of the Anglo-Newfoundland Development Company. Lord Northcliffe himself had a house in Grand Falls.

The people of Newfoundland, and especially the citizens of St. John's, were caught up in the transatlantic fever. The war had brought the country into closer contact with the outside world. Many of her young men had gone overseas, for Newfoundland's contribution to the war effort, in terms of manpower, had been great in relation to her size. As would be expected of a seafaring nation, most of these young men had served in the Royal Navy, but in addition they had fought with distinction in the British Army. The 'first five hundred' left for England a few weeks after the outbreak of war, to form the first battalion of the Newfoundland Regiment. As part of the famous 29th Division they took part in the Gallipoli campaign, and for their distinguished service were granted the title of 'Royal' by King George V. The Royal Newfoundland Regiment later fought on the Somme, and suffered heavy casualties at Beaumont Hamel on July 1st, 1916. Of them, Sir Douglas Haig wrote: 'Their courage and devotion to duty on this day has never been surpassed.'

The cap-badge of the Royal Newfoundland Regiment is the caribou's head, and in Bowring Park, on the outskirts of St. John's, there is a memorial to the Regiment. A bronze caribou, life size, stands with its head uplifted, on an outcrop of natural rock, surrounded by pine-trees. It is one of the finest war-memorials to be seen anywhere in the world, and a second and similar one, for which the rocks and pine trees were brought from Newfoundland, stands at the spot at Beaumont Hamel where so many Newfoundlanders lost their lives.

In the spring of 1919 the men of Newfoundland were returning from the war. They found themselves back among people who were once again enjoying the sensation of being at the centre of world interest, as the press of every continent turned its attention to the preparations going on at St. John's. The city seemed to be full of aviators and newspaper reporters, who made their headquarters at the Cochrane Hotel, where Marconi had stayed eighteen years before. The shopkeepers vied with each other to produce window-displays with an aviation theme, and the newspapers carried advertisements which used the same idea. Every day lumber-wagons drawn by teams of horses struggled up the steep streets from the waterfront, laden with huge crates containing parts of aircraft, often necessitating the removal of fencing or parts of front gardens at awkward spots.

The first aviators to arrive were Harry Hawker and his navigator, Mackenzie-Grieve. They landed at St. John's on March 29th, bringing with them their crated Sopwith *Atlantic*, and after a brief reconnaissance settled down at Glendenning's Farm, about six miles out of St. John's. They were followed on April 11th by Freddy Raynham and C. W. F. Morgan with the smaller Rolls-Martinsyde *Raymor*. The S.S. *Digby* bringing them was unable to enter St. John's because of ice and they were landed at Placentia, arriving in the capital by train two days later. They chose for their airfield a space to the north of Quidi Vidi Lake, later to become an American Army base in the second world war, and now known as Fort Peperell. Here they put up a canvas hangar and started to erect their plane.

The largest party was the Handley Page group, 100 strong with their V/1500 bomber. They moved out to Harbour Grace, sixty miles away, much to the indignation of the citizens of St. John's,

32 Marconi, Kemp and Paget inside Cabot Tower

33 Preparing to fly one of the aerial kites on Signal Hill

34 Sir Cavendish Boyle (Governor), Sir Robert Bond (Prime Minister), and members of the Cabinet, with Marconi, December 17th, 1901

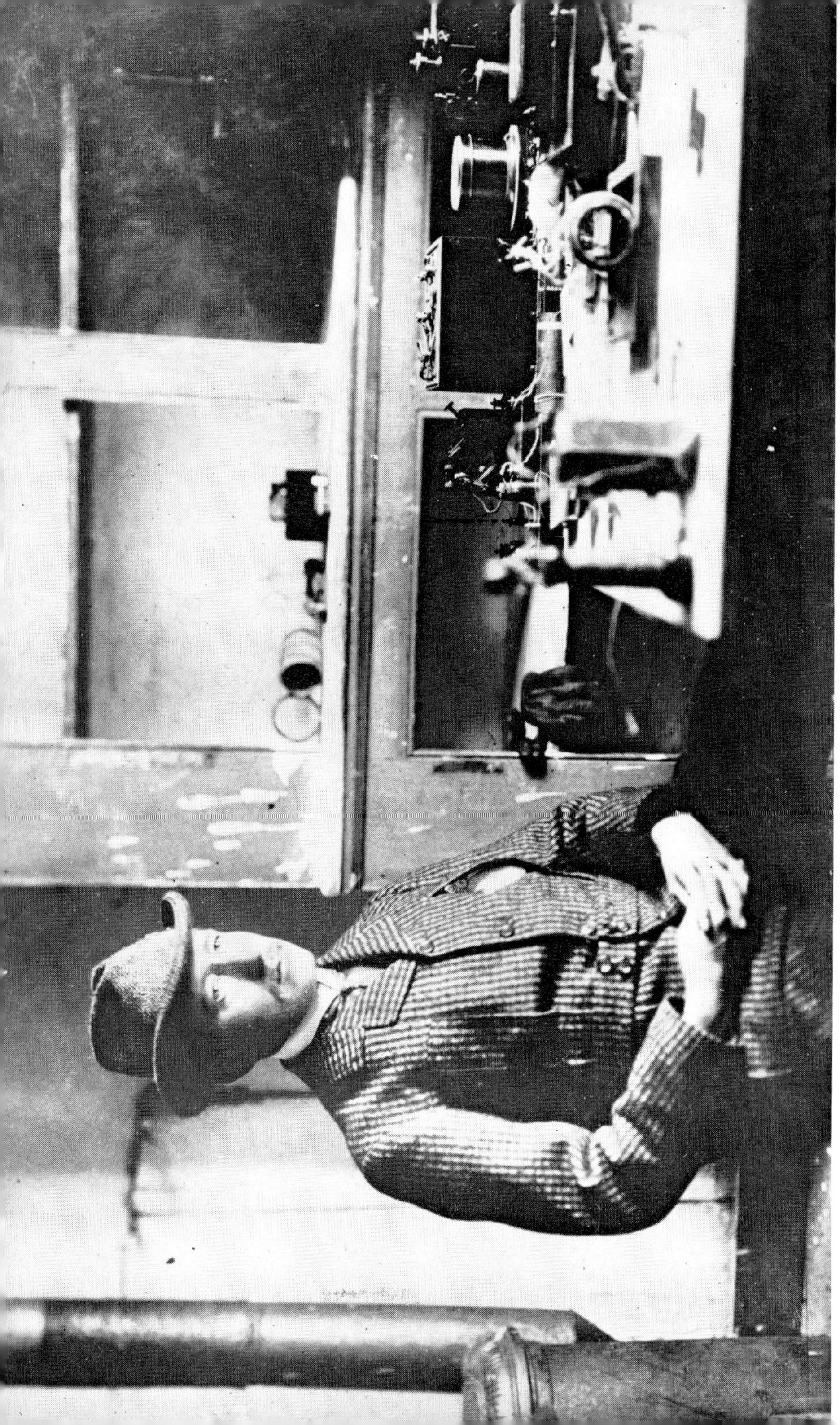

36 Marconi Memorial, Signal Hill, St. John's

37 The Vickers *Vimy* at Lester's Field before the transatlantic flight

38 Alcock and Brown taking off from Lester's Field, June 14th, 1919

39 The statue of Sir John Alcock and Sir Arthur Whitten Brown at London Airport

who since the days of Marconi had considered that the capital city ought to have a monopoly of transatlantic endeavours.

Last of all the airmen to arrive were Alcock and Brown. They came in advance of their main party and their aeroplane, and had little to do while the other parties were preparing for their attempts. They put up at the Cochrane Hotel, and while awaiting the arrival of their plane searched the countryside for a suitable airfield.

The general interest was heightened by the arrival in St. John's harbour, early in May, of the U.S.S. *Chicago*, and by the news that she had come to make preparations for two separate attempts by the United States Navy to fly the Atlantic. Theirs was an independent effort, which had been planned for some time, and was not connected with the *Daily Mail* contest. They had no intention of making a direct crossing, but were to fly to Europe by stages, via the Azores. The main attempt was to be made by three Curtiss flying boats, the N.C.-1, 3, and 4, flying from Trepassey Bay, some eighty miles to the south of St. John's.

The name Trepassey, with its suggestion of Cornwall, is yet another reminder of the strong connection between Newfoundland and the West Country of England, from whence came many of the island's settlers. Trepassey is at the extreme south-eastern corner of Newfoundland, close to one of the main Atlantic sea-routes, and in the past the rocky coast thereabouts has been the cause of many shipwrecks. The inhabitants of Trepassey, like many of their Cornish forbears, at one time augumented their earnings from fishing by 'salvage' operations on the wrecks. Some of the older members of the community have been known to complain of such modern inventions as radio direction-finding which have largely put an end to these activities.

In May 1919 a number of United States Navy destroyers arrived in Trepassey Bay. The first of them excited the professional interest of the local inhabitants by running aground, but no doubt to their disappointment was soon refloated. Shortly afterwards the three seaplanes arrived and made ready for their Atlantic flight. They were to be supported by five cruisers and sixty destroyers, spaced out at regular intervals across the ocean to the Azores. This was to be the first attempt for which the *Chicago* had arrived in preparation. The other attempt, which was to take place from St. John's, was by a lighter-than-air machine, the United States Navy C.-5, their latest

L

non-rigid airship. It was quite a small 'blimp' of only 170,000 cubic feet capacity, and at first its attempt was not taken seriously. However, it arrived at St. John's on May 15th having flown the 1,400 miles from its base at Montauk without incident. Its commander, Lieutenant-Commander E. W. Coil, announced his intention of taking off for Ireland as soon as the weather was suitable.

The weather, however, was proving the biggest difficulty for all the flyers. It was imperative that conditions should be just right, as the aircraft used had little margin of safety. But that year the spring was late in coming and throughout March and April the winter gales persisted. The flyers waited and waited in vain for some fine weather. When the C-5 landed at St. John's beside Quidi Vidi Lake on May 15th, at 11 a.m., however, the weather was for once calm. Lieutenant-Commander Coil and his second in command, Lieutenant Lawrence, went aboard the *Chicago* in St. John's Harbour to get a few hours' sleep while the airship was refuelled and provisions put aboard.

While this was going on the wind began to get up. The blimp strained at its mooring ropes, and all the hands available had to hang on to them to prevent the airship being carried away. To the officers in charge, however, it seemed that the wind, which was blowing from the west, might be just what the vessel required to make a fast getaway on its flight. Accordingly, word was sent to Coil and Lawrence who were routed out of their bunks and came hurrying ashore. Before they had arrived, however, a gust of sixty miles an hour picked up the airship and flung it down, damaging the control car and a propeller. Any attempt to take off was now impossible, and Lieut. Little, the officer in charge, attempted to pull the rip panel and let out the gas, so that the ship could be saved and the flight resumed in a few days' time. Before he could do so, however, a strong gust of wind carried the blimp into the air again, and to save the ground crew from being carried away the order was given to release the ropes. The C-5, without a crew, leaped into the air and vanished out to sea. She was never seen again. By a narrow mischance she missed a very good opportunity of being the first aircraft to cross the Atlantic.

The St. John's shopkeepers changed their window displays, and pictures of British Bulldogs with Union Jacks appeared accompanied by such slogans as 'what we have, we hold'. The United States Navy had not long to wait, however, for its moment of triumph, for on the following day, May 16th, the three seaplanes took off from Trepassey Bay for the Azores. In charge of the flight was Commander John H. Towers, in N.C.-3. Each seaplane carried a crew of five, and 15 pounds of food and drink per man.

They did not fly in formation, but soon separated. Some 300 miles from the Azores, the first casualty occurred. A thick fog had come down, and Lieutenant-Commander Bellinger in N.C.-1, fearing the possibility of crashing into a mountainside, decided to land on the sea. In doing so he misjudged, and damaged the seaplane, which began to sink. Fortunately a British steamship, the *Iona*, was close by, and all the crew were picked up safely. A further hundred miles on, the N.C.-3, with Commander Towers, had to make a forced landing on the ocean. This time there was no ship to receive them, but by means of alternate sailing and taxiing they managed to cover the 200 miles to Ponta Delgada, in the Azores, taking fifty-two hours to do it.

The remaining seaplane, N.C.-4, piloted by Lieutenant-Commander Read, reached the Azores safely, after a journey of fifteen hours. A few days later it flew on to Britain and landed at Plymouth on May 31st, 1919—the first aircraft to fly the Atlantic, though not in one direct flight as required by the *Daily Mail* contest.

The news of the Americans' success reached St. John's on Saturday, May 17th, at tea-time. Hawker and Mackenzie-Grieve and Raynham and Morgan, who had been waiting at St. John's for over a month until the weather would allow them to take off, felt that they could no longer delay. If they got away immediately, they could reach Britain while the American seaplanes were still at the Azores. Their impatience ran high, and it was fortunate for them that the weather reports were at last favourable. In their anxiety to be off, they might have risked flying even in bad weather conditions.

On Sunday, May 17th, the Sopwith *Atlantic* stood ready outside its hangar at Glendenning's Farm. It was a relatively small machine, built, like the *Raymor*, specially for the Atlantic crossing. Its design and construction were carried out in the space of six weeks, an amazing performance when measured by modern standards. The Sopwith firm, which produced it, had become famous during the war as builders of the *Pup* and *Camel* fighter planes. The *Atlantic* was a two-seater biplane, powered by a single Rolls-Royce Eagle engine of 360 horse-power. Its cruising speed was 100 miles an hour, and it carried sufficient fuel for thirty hours' flying. The undercarriage could be dropped after take-off, thus increasing speed by seven miles an hour. The top half of the fuselage was designed like a boat, which could be detached and launched if a forced landing were made in the sea. Hawker and Grieve had practised boating in it on a pond near Glendenning's Farm.

The pilot, Harry Hawker, an Australian, was one of the most brilliant pilots in Britain. Rejected by the Royal Flying Corps on medical grounds, he had spent all the war years as chief test pilot of the Sopwith Company and had an impressive record of flying to his credit. His navigator, Lieutenant-Commander Mackenzie-Grieve, R.N., had been navigating officer of H.M.S. *Campania*, the Royal Navy's seaplane depot-ship, and had been released from duty by the Service to take part in the flight.

There were few people at Glendenning's Farm to see them off at 3.48 p.m. that Sunday afternoon. With a strong headwind they took the air easily, and passed over the city of St. John's, close to the house in which, 1,000 feet below, the author of this book was asleep in his cot. Just after passing over the coast they dropped their undercarriage in the sea (it was later picked up by a fisherman, and is now exhibited in St. John's museum) and then climbed rapidly until they were out of sight of the crowds watching in St. John's.

Meanwhile, at Quidi Vidi Lake preparations were going on to get Raynham and Morgan's machine ready for flight. As soon as they knew that Hawker and Grieve had taken off they decided to follow suit. They had a faster plane, and it was still quite possible for them to overtake the others and win the prize.

As the news spread round the city by that mysterious kind of grapevine which always comes into play on such occasions, the Sunday afternoon crowds poured out of town, down the Kingsbridge road to Quidi Vidi. It was almost like a second regatta-day. The rumour had spread around that this afternoon it would be no mere test-flight, and as the crowds saw Hawker and Grieve's Sopwith pass overhead and drop its wheels the rumour was confirmed, and excitement grew.

For once the newspaper reporters were caught on the hop, not knowing whether to make for Glendenning's Farm, six miles away, or for Quidi Vidi Lake. They couldn't be at both. As a result, most of them chose Quidi Vidi.

As the crowds gathered, they saw the red and yellow Rolls-Martinsyde machine wheeled out of its hangar. Like the Sopwith plane, it had been specially built for this contest, and was quite distinct from the monoplane which the Martinsyde firm had produced for the 1914 attempt.* It was a two-seater biplane, powered by a Rolls-Royce Falcon engine and able to carry enough fuel for twenty-five hours' flying. The curious-sounding name 'Raymor' was compounded of the first three letters of the surnames of its crew, Raynham and Morgan.

The two airmen took their places, the engine was started up, and with a roar the aircraft sped down the field. Then, just as the wheels had left the ground, a violent gust of wind caught it from the side. It tipped, and one wing caught the ground, and suddenly the plane dived and hit the field in a cloud of dust. The spectators rushed forward, but to their relief the two airmen climbed out of their cockpits apparently uninjured. It was found, however, that Morgan had been badly hurt. He had been flung forward against the compass, a piece of glass entering his head. He was quickly removed to hospital. For a time, at least, the Rolls-Martinsyde was out of the contest. Eventually the plane was repaired and renamed "Chimera" and Raynham found another navigator. He tried again a month later, but again crashed.

At the Cochrane Hotel that night the atmosphere was more subdued than usual, and the feeling grew throughout the next twenty-four hours. Everyone listened for the telephone, anxiously awaiting news of Hawker and Grieve. The flyers carried a wireless set in the plane, and at the start of the flight were in touch, for a short time, with the Royal Navy's station at Mount Pearl, just outside St. John's. After that, however, nothing more had been heard. The hours dragged on and still no news came through. By Monday night it was obvious that all was not well. The only hope was that the flyers had come down in the sea and had been rescued. The people of St. John's,

---

* The firm which built it was formed in 1908 as 'Martin & Handasyde', and started production in the first hangar at Brooklands flying ground. During the first world war, under the name of Martinsyde, the firm produced their well-known F-4 single seater fighter. Mr. G. H. Handasyde, who designed these early planes, died in 1958. Another designer for the firm was Sidney Camm, who designed the immortal *Hurricane* of Battle of Britain fame in World War II.

who had long been accustomed to losses at sea, tried to keep up spirits by recounting the many instances when men had been rescued after all hope had been given up. But it must have been a cheerless business for the remaining members of the Sopwith party as they dismantled their hangar and packed up their equipment for the return journey. Nor was it much happier for the Martinsyde people as they set about salvaging their plane.

In Britain, where the news of the take-off had been received with tremendous excitement, anxiety grew as the flyers became overdue. On Tuesday the newspapers announced that Hawker and Grieve must be presumed lost, and criticism was turned on the British Government. Apart from sending a meteorological officer to St. John's to advise on suitable weather conditions, and placing the Naval wireless station at Mount Pearl at the flyers' disposal, the Government had considered the flights to be purely private affairs, and had treated them accordingly. This was contrasted with the elaborate preparations made by the United States Government for their own flyers, though these, of course, had carried out their flights as part of normal service duty in the U.S. Navy.

When Hawker and Grieve climbed over St. John's and headed out to sea, they found weather conditions ideal for flying. For four hours they flew steadily onwards at 10,000 feet, without anything eventful happening. With the wind behind them they made good progress.

About 500 miles out in the Atlantic they ran into cumulus cloud. First it began to rain, and then it froze. To make matters worse, the engine temperature began to rise above the safe limit. There seemed to be nothing to account for this, and as the temperature went on mounting, Hawker did the only thing possible, and shutting off the engine, put the aircraft into a long dive. At the end of it he started up the engine again and climbed. In this way he kept going, the engine cooling down on the dives and heating up again as he climbed. They left the cloud and travelled on in calm weather.

All night they flew on like this, until at sunrise they ran into a vast area of cumulo-nimbus, in which the machine was tossed to and fro by turbulence. For no apparent reason the engine stopped, and after frantic efforts by Hawker was restarted only twenty feet from the surface of the sea. By now things were getting desperate, the water in the cooling system was boiling, and little of it was left. They decided to turn south and fly across the shipping routes looking for a vessel. They did this, zig-zagging across the probable path of shipping, until, with the engine at its last gasp they sighted a small steamship. They circled around it, firing Very signals, and then dropped into the sea just ahead of it. The 'boat' section of the aeroplane was launched and Hawker and Grieve took their places in it.

The sea was so rough that it was two hours before they were picked up, and found themselves on board the Danish tramp-steamer *Mary*. Their first request to the captain was to radio news of their arrival. But the *Mary* had no wireless, and so for nearly a week news of their rescue did not reach the world.

On Sunday, May 25th, exactly a week after the flyers had taken off from St. John's the lighthouse keepers at the Butt of Lewis on the West coast of Scotland saw a small steamship making in to the shore and signalling to them. It was the *Mary* and she passed the news that she had on board Hawker and Grieve. The news was flashed on to London and passed on to those concerned. Hawker's wife heard it just as she was leaving church. The following day it was front page news in all the papers.

Hawker and Mackenzie-Grieve landed in Scotland and travelled up to London. When they got to King's Cross Station there was a crowd of 10,000 people to greet them. Among them was a group of Australian soldiers eager to greet their fellow-countryman, Harry Hawker. The Royal Aero Club had sent a car to the station to meet the flyers, but as soon as they entered it the Aussies gathered around it, lifted it shoulder high, and carried it through the streets. Everywhere the two men received a tremendous reception, and the *Daily Mail* announced that although they had not completed the crossing, they would receive a consolation prize of £5,000. Meanwhile the original offer still held good.

It is not difficult to imagine the relief with which the news was received at St. John's. The ensuing celebration at the Cochrane Hotel is remembered to this day.

Ten days after the rescue the wreckage of the Sopwith *Atlantic* was found, still afloat, by the American freighter *Lake Charlotteville*. It was rescued from the sea and brought to England, where it was exhibited to the public on the roof of Selfridge's store in Oxford Street. The bag of mail which it carried was rescued with it, and delivered to the Post Office for distribution, the first transatlantic airmail to be carried. It was found, on examination, that the shutters of the engine radiator were closed, which led to the conjecture that this had been the cause of the overheating.

Harry Hawker, it is sad to relate, did not live long to enjoy his triumph. After surviving his crash in the Atlantic he was killed shortly afterwards in a flying accident, on a test flight.

So, in Newfoundland, for a short time, the activities of aviators and reporters were lessened. At Harbour Grace the Handley Page party were still busy making their preparations, but at St. John's only Alcock and Brown were left in the running, and they still had no aircraft.

CHAPTER 9

Alcock and Brown Win the Prize

BY THE END of May 1919, St. John's had temporarily recovered from the excitement of the last two weeks. The United States Navy had returned home; Harry Hawker was safe and in London; Freddy Raynham was recovering from his crash while his aeroplane was repaired and another navigator sought, and for a time the aviation fever that had gripped everyone subsided.

But no one had yet achieved a direct crossing of the Atlantic, and the *Daily Mail* £10,000 prize was still to be won. Two as yet untried contestants still waited in Newfoundland. At Harbour Grace Admiral Mark Kerr's Handley Page team were still working to get their giant four-engined V.1500 ready for flight, while at St. John's Alcock and Brown were starting to assemble their Vickers *Vimy* newly arrived from England.

They had been the last to enter the contest, and the last to arrive in Newfoundland. When Hawker and Raynham had each made their attempt, and when the American seaplanes had reached the Azores, Alcock and Brown were still waiting for their *Vimy* to arrive from England; airmen without an aircraft in the midst of all the excitement and hubbub. Yet they persevered and went on to win the prize. It would be hard to find a better example of the fable of the tortoise and the hare.

Like all the other pilots competing, Jack Alcock was a young man when he flew the Atlantic. He was born in 1892 in Manchester, and from early on in life flying was an absorbing interest for him. He was trained as an engineer, but his one ambition was to fly. His chance came in 1912, when the firm for which he worked were asked to repair an aeroplane engine for a famous French aviator, Maurice Ducrocq. After working on it, Alcock went down to Brooklands to install it, and Ducrocq was so pleased with his work that he took him on as his mechanic.

At Brooklands Alcock was in his element. He found himself among flying enthusiasts like himself—young men from all walks of life, who lived and talked nothing but aeroplanes, and whose one ambition was to fly. At that time Brooklands was the centre of the flying industry; most of the aviation companies had their works situated there, around the famous motor-racing track in the middle of which was the aerodrome.

Before long Alcock got a chance to fly. He learnt, as did everyone at that time, by being thrown in at the deep end. There were no such things as dual controls, and after a short spell of instruction on the ground the would-be pilot was sent up solo to fend for himself.

Alcock met, and made friends with, two of his future competitors, Freddy Raynham and Harry Hawker, the Australian. The three soon became well known as outstanding pilots of this pre-war period. Much of their time was spent taking part in the many flying meetings and races which were held at Hendon, in North London, and to which the public flocked in their thousands every week-end.

On the outbreak of war he joined the Royal Naval Air Service but the Admiralty considered him too valuable to fly operationally, and so he found himself busy training pilots. After a year he was put in charge of a school of acrobatic flying, with the rank of Flight Sub-Lieutenant. At last, in 1916 he got his wish and a transfer to a squadron in the Eastern Mediterranean, based at Mudros. Here he had twelve months of operational flying in all types of aircraft, including the big Handley Page O.400 which had been sent out to bomb Constantinople. It came abruptly to an end when his plane made a forced landing while on a raid, and he and his crew were made prisoners by the Turks.

Throughout the weary months of his captivity Alcock passed the time making plans for an attempt on the *Daily Mail* transatlantic prize, as soon as the war was over. He had a good idea of the kind of aircraft he would use; it would be a bomber like the O.400.

The end of the war came, and on his return home Alcock set about putting his plans into action. As soon as he had been demobilised he approached the Vickers company and offered his services as a pilot. By this time the other companies had their preparations well in hand, but the Vickers people, although they had a first-class competitor in the *Vimy*, a long-range bomber, had done little towards taking part in the *Daily Mail* contest. A visit to their works by Alcock was sufficient to kindle their enthusiasm, and with the management on his side a race against time began to get the machine ready.

The Vickers *Vimy* was a long-distance bomber, designed by Rex Pierson for the specific purpose of bombing Berlin. It was too late to be used for this objective, and when the first twelve had been completed production was suspended. Now work was started again on the thirteenth, but fortunately Alcock was not superstitious.

The *Vimy* was a twin-engined biplane, with a range of 2,440 miles. Powered by two Rolls-Royce Eagle Mark VIII engines, each of 360 horse-power, it had a top speed of 100 miles per hour. It was 42·7 feet long, and had a wing-span of 68 feet. The four-bladed propellers were of wood, and the fuselage and wings of wood covered with fabric. Some modifications were made in the course of construction. The bombing gear and armament were of course omitted, and the bomb-bays filled with extra petrol tanks. Instead of two separate cockpits, one larger one, in which pilot and navigator could sit side by side, was fitted. A full size model of this cockpit can be seen in the Science Museum at South Kensington, and it is not difficult to visualise the cramped conditions in which the flyers spent the sixteen hours of their crossing—in itself a feat of considerable endurance. Other modifications to the plane consisted of the fitting of a wheel in place of a nose skid and the fitting of a petrol tank specially designed to act as a buoyancy chamber.

Alcock spent all his time supervising the erection of the *Vimy*, but as it began to approach completion he gave much thought to the question of a navigator, for which post no one had yet been found. The end of March had come; Hawker and Mackenzie Grieve had already arrived in Newfoundland and the matter was becoming urgent.

At this moment there appeared on the scene, for the first time, Arthur Whitten Brown. The son of an American engineer who had come to Manchester to build a factory for the Westinghouse Company, Arthur was born in Glasgow in 1886 and was thus Alcock's senior by six years. Like him, he had been trained as an engineer, in his father's works in Manchester. But although the two men had been brought up in the same city they never met until the Atlantic flight brought them together.

When the war came Brown was in South Africa. Although technically an American citizen he returned to Britain and enlisted in the Army, being gazetted second lieutenant in the Manchester Regiment. After service on the Western Front he applied for a transfer to the

Royal Flying Corps. In due course he became an observer and made many flights spotting for the artillery and taking photographs. He became interested in the art of navigation and spent much of his time studying the subject, which at that time was in its infancy, as far as its application to air travel was concerned. The early flyers navigated by following roads or railways, and when Blériot flew the Channel in 1910 he did not carry a map, but just pointed his nose in the direction of Dover.

In November 1916 Brown's plane, while on a reconnaissance flight, was forced down by German fighters, and crashed behind the enemy lines. Brown's left leg was severely injured, and he and his pilot were taken prisoner.

Throughout the next two years he passed the time furthering his study of navigation. But now his interest was not simply academic. Like another prisoner of war, he had always at the front of his mind the thought of Lord Northcliffe's £10,000 prize. Whoever won it would need a first-class navigator, and Arthur Whitten Brown was determined that he would be that navigator.

The war ended and Brown was demobilised, and in common with thousands of other ex-servicemen looking for a job. But jobs were scarce, and he found himself making one depressing journey after another to engineering firms in search of employment, before he finally came to Vickers. He had no idea that they were preparing an entry for the *Daily Mail* contest, and it was purely by chance that his interest in air navigation came out in his interview. As soon as it was known, however, the works manager sent him round to see Alcock. The two of them started to discuss the proposed flight, and before Brown left the Vickers works he had been offered, and had accepted, the post of navigator. Unexpectedly his dream had come true.

Thus it was that on Tuesday, May 13th, 1919, Alcock and Brown found themselves standing together on the station platform at St. John's, having just arrived from Halifax via Port-aux-Basques and the Newfoundland Railway. Two more different personalities it would be hard to imagine, as one glance at a photograph of the pair is enough to show. Alcock was big, bluff, and boisterous, the life and soul of every party he found himself in; an extrovert whose life was centred around flying; who was never happier than when he was in the cockpit of a plane, and to whom flying was an end in itself. Brown, on the other hand was slight in appearance, quiet and reserved in manner, and studious by nature. He read widely, and his interest in flying was one of many interests. Yet it was these wide differences of character that made the two men an ideal team for this project; they were complementary to each other, but never antagonistic.

On arrival they put up at the Cochrane Hotel where they found Raynham and Hawker with the others of their parties. Both were ready to go, and simply waiting for suitable weather. So, too, were the American flyers at Trepassey. To Alcock and Brown, whose aircraft was still somewhere on the Atlantic with its mechanics, it must have been galling to see all the preparations going on around them, and be unable to do anything. They spent the time searching for a suitable airfield, and soon realised that this was going to be a big problem. The Avalon peninsula, on which St. John's is situated, is rocky and hilly. There is little flat ground anywhere near St. John's. The modern airport at Torbay, which serves the city today, was built only with considerable effort by the United States Army during the second world war, for military purposes. Alcock and Brown soon came to realise that the only two possible airstrips had already been rented by the Sopwith and Martinsyde parties. This was a difficulty they had not foreseen.

It was solved temporarily after the unsuccessful attempt of Raynham and Morgan. Realising that it would be some weeks before he could make another attempt, Freddy Raynham very generously offered the use of his airfield at Quidi Vidi, and Alcock accepted it gratefully. It would provide a place where the *Vimy* could be assembled, and from which it could make a test flight. For take-off with the full load of fuel required for the Atlantic crossing, a much larger runway would be required.

Sunday, May 26th, brought two items of good news to Brown and Alcock. First came the tidings that the S.S. *Glendavon*, carrying the *Vimy* and the rest of their party, would be docking the next morning; then, in the evening came the great news for all the flyers that Hawker and Mackenzie Grieve had been picked up and were safe.

The next morning they were down at the harbour early to meet the boat. Alcock had arranged with Mr. Lester, a haulage contractor, to get the crates containing the aircraft to Quidi Vidi, and soon teams of straining horses were making their way up Water Street and out along the Kingsbridge Road. As soon as they arrived at the airfield mechanics got to work uncrating and erecting the *Vimy*. It was too big to go into Raynham's canvas hangar, and so all work had to be carried out in the open in the cold, wet weather that still prevailed. All hands worked at top speed, however, conscious all the time of the Handley Page challenge. Several times the big V.1500, piloted by Major Brackley, passed over St. John's on a test flight. Each time the party at Quidi Vidi paused to look at it and then breathed sighs of relief as it turned and flew back to Harbour Grace.

Work on the *Vimy* went on at top speed. Brown himself installed the wireless and the navigational instruments, while Alcock supervised the assembly of the aircraft. Work was proceeding well, but there was still the worry of finding an airfield. The country around St. John's was scoured without success, and then, when Alcock was considering approaching the Handley Page party at Harbour Grace to see if he could negotiate the use of their airfield, he had a visit from Mr. Lester, the haulage contractor, who offered him the use of a field in which he kept his horses. Alcock went with him to see it. Lester's Field, as it was afterwards known, is situated by Munday's Pond, at the west end of St. John's. At first sight it did not appear too promising. A stone dyke ran across it, while trees and boulders were dotted about. There was sufficient room, however, and Lester promised to help in clearing the land. Moreover, he offered the use of it without payment. So on the next day work started, with the help of as many as could be spared from Alcock's party. The boulders were dynamited, trees uprooted, and the dyke torn down. Within a week a passable airstrip had been prepared 500 yards long.

On June 9th the *Vimy* was ready for its test flight, but before it could take the air a new problem arose. It was found that the supply of petrol which they had brought was unsuitable. It had been stored in rubber-lined metal containers, and the rubber had dissolved, making the petrol useless as fuel. Again Freddy Raynham came to the rescue, and sportingly lent sufficient fuel for the test flight. The *Vimy* behaved perfectly, took off in the 500 yds available, and circled St. John's several times before landing on its new airstrip at Lester's Field. A day or two later further supplies of petrol arrived, and all that they now needed was suitable weather. In spite of their late start they had put themselves, by sheer hard work, into the running for the *Daily Mail* prize.

Now, like Hawker and Raynham before them, they waited and

waited for the right weather. Each day Flight-Lieutenant Clements, the meteorologist who had been sent out by the R.A.F. to assist the flyers, gave them his report. Each day they had to put off their flight. If the weather was fine in Newfoundland, there were storms in mid-Atlantic. When the weather over the Atlantic was calm, there was fog on the Banks and over St. John's. Day after day they made all their preparations and then had to return to the hotel. The only consolation was that their competitors at Harbour Grace were in the same position.

At last, on June 14th, Lieutenant Clements was able to give them a favourable report. It was a calm morning after two days of gale-force winds, and the *Vimy* stood waiting, ready for the long trip. Every possible precaution had been taken; on Alcock's instruction every drop of water in the cooling system had been boiled and filtered. He was taking no chances after what had happened to Harry Hawker. Eight hundred and seventy gallons of petrol and forty gallons of oil had been pumped by hand into the tanks, the wireless had been tested with Mount Pearl station, and all Brown's charts and navigating instruments put aboard. For their own sustenance on the journey the two men relied upon sandwiches and beer, chocolate, and hot coffee. One of their last acts was to lash to a strut by the cockpit Alcock's mascot, a stuffed toy cat, known as 'Lucky Jim'. This gave rise to a newspaper report, sometimes quoted in accounts of the crossing, that they carried a live black cat with them for luck. Anyone who has seen the cockpit of the *Vimy* would be unlikely to believe this story; not only was there insufficient space to swing the proverbial cat, but there was not even enough room to stow one.

June 14th was a Saturday, and from midday onwards the crowds began to gather at Lester's Field as word was passed around by the 'grapevine' that the flight was on. They brought picnics with them and prepared to make a holiday of it. During the morning Alcock and Brown had been waiting for the wind to veer round to the right direction, and by one o'clock it had done so. They finished their lunch and climbed into the cockpit. Among those who had come to see them off was Sir Michael Cashin, the Prime Minister, and Dr. Robinson, Postmaster-General, who handed over a small bag of mail for them to carry. Lieutenant Clements, acting as starter for the Royal Aero Club, fixed the Club's official seal on the side of the fuselage.

At 1.24 the engines were started up, and a few minutes later, in obedience to Alcock's signal, the mechanics whipped away the wheel chocks (aircraft brakes were still a thing of the future). The huge ungainly shape of the *Vimy* commenced to move, jolting over the rough ground, and gathering speed until she rose from the ground at exactly 1.45 p.m. by Newfoundland time, amid the cheers of the crowd. Alcock flew inland for some minutes to gain height, then made a wide turn and flew over St. John's at 1,000 feet. They roared over the harbour, past the Cabot Tower on Signal Hill, over the Narrows, and out to sea. One more attempt to fly the Atlantic had started.

They crossed the coast of Newfoundland at 1,200 feet, and reported the fact by wireless to Mount Pearl. All went well, and after half an hour they encountered a strong following wind which pushed them along at a steady 140 knots. Throttled down, the two Rolls-Royce engines purred happily away, and the flyers felt that they had made a good start.

Back at Lester's Field the crowds began to depart, and in an inevitable atmosphere of anticlimax the Vickers mechanics set about the task of packing up their equipment. Some of the party went to the wireless station at Mount Pearl to await any messages from the flyers. Lieutenant Clements cabled to the Royal Aero Club to inform them officially that Alcock and Brown had started their transatlantic flight at 16.13 hours Greenwich Mean Time, and the newspaper reporters besieged the cable office to get off their stories.

An hour after leaving the *Vimy* ran into thick fog. Brown had no way of checking their position except the inaccurate one of dead reckoning. He urged Alcock to climb, in order to get above the fog and for nearly an hour they did so, until at last they came into the open. It was now 18.00 hours, and Brown tried to get in touch with Mount Pearl again, to give his estimated position. He was unable to do so, and found, on checking, that the small propeller that drove the dynamo supplying current to the transmitter had broken. They still had a receiver, but no more messages could be sent. Worse still, the dynamo also supplied the current for their electrically heated flying suits. From now on the cold would be intense.

Hardly had they discovered this misfortune, when one much more frightening occurred. A sudden loud noise from their starboard engine caused them to look round and see flames streaming from it. A section of exhaust pipe had come away close to the manifold, but fortunately the flames were clear of any part of the aircraft. They flew on with the exhaust making a deafening noise in their ears, and from then on all communication had to be by written notes.

At 19.40 hours they were flying in cloud at 5,000 feet. Brown reckoned that they had covered 450 miles, and it had become necessary for him to top up the main petrol tanks by hand-pumping from the reserve. Still he had had no opportunity to get a sight of the sun by which he could check his position, and having no way of calculating wind or drift he was getting worried about this.

At last, a hour later, they came out of the cloud at 6,000 feet. For ten minutes only the sun shone on them, but that was enough for Brown to get a sight with his sextant. He was pleased to find, as a result of his calculations, that his dead reckoning was not far out and they were only a few miles to the south of their Great Circle course. Then the cloud came down again and they flew on blindly.

Both men were beginning to suffer from their cramped positions, Alcock because he could not for one instant relax his grip on the controls, and Brown because his wounded leg was giving him pain. Their electrically heated suits had up till now kept warm from the battery, but with no dynamo to keep it charged this now gave out. Darkness came on and still they flew onwards in dense cloud, until at last, just after midnight, they flew out into a wonderful clear night sky. A full moon shone down on them, illuminating the masses of cotton-wool cloud below, across which the shadow of the Vimy slowly moved, and above them the stars shone brightly.

Brown took a sight of the Pole Star and worked out their position. This in itself was quite a feat, in the cramped quarters of the cockpit. Not for him the chart table and adjustable reading lamp of a navigator on a modern transatlantic plane. He had to balance his books on one knee and scribble his calculations on a pad strapped to his other knee, by the light of a torch held in one hand. He found that they had flown a distance of 850 nautical miles, and had thus covered almost half the distance between Newfoundland and Ireland. They marked the occasion with a meal of sandwiches and coffee, laced with whisky to keep out the cold. Outside the cockpit the temperature was below zero, and the electrically heated suits had now failed. All

M

around them the banks and pillars of clouds gleamed in the moonlight, and the loneliness was intense.

One advantage of flying the Atlantic from west to east is that nights are short. At 03.10 hours the flyers saw the darkness begin to give way to the dawn, though in Newfoundland it was only just after midnight. Suddenly the flyers emerged from a small cloud to see ahead of them a huge mass of cumulo-nimbus. There was no time to alter course, and the aircraft flew right into the middle of it. It was caught by sudden turbulence, and thrown around like an autumn leaf. In the cockpit the two flyers pitched around like shuttlecocks, held in their seats only by the safety belts. Hail beat on the aeroplane and lightning played all around it. Then speed dropped, and the *Vimy* stalled and commenced to spiral down towards the Atlantic. Alcock struggled with the controls, but he had lost all sense of balance, and the lightning dazzled him so that he could not see the instruments. From 4,000 feet they dropped quickly to 1,000 then only 100. At 60 feet they came out of the storm and Alcock saw the waves below him. He just had time to right the aircraft and they found themselves flying so close to the sea that they felt the spray on the underside of the *Vimy*. Not surprisingly it was some minutes before they recovered themselves, glanced at the compass, and found that they were flying westwards back to Newfoundland.

They turned and flew onwards, gradually climbing, now that the storm was past. Once more the routine of flying was resumed; petrol pumped, dead reckoning checked and engine readings taken. Before long, however, another danger threatened. It started to rain, and as they tried to fly above it the rain turned to snow. The surface of the aircraft began to ice up, and the two engines began to labour. Brown looked and saw that the air intakes were being blocked up with snow. If something were not done to clear them the engines would soon give up.

There was only one possible thing to do. He released his safety belt and climbed out of the cockpit on to the wing. With his crippled leg and the ice on wings and struts it was a precarious journey, but he reached the port engine safely. Holding on grimly against the slipstream and the 100 mile an hour wind, he cleared the air intake of snow and fought his way back. The engine picked up and resumed its normal note.

They were 9,000 feet above the Atlantic, and with the snow still beating against him, Brown repeated his hazardous undertaking on the starboard side, until at last both engines were running smoothly again. But that was not the end of it; the snow continued, and before they flew out of it Brown had to repeat his performance five times.

At length, at 07.20 hours they came out of the storm at 11,000 feet. For the last time a sight of the sun enabled them to fix their position, and this time they found themselves within a few hundred miles of Ireland. The worst ordeal was over, but all was not yet plain sailing. Scarcely had Brown got his sight, when one of the engines began to misfire. The controls were also becoming so iced up that they could scarcely be moved, and Alcock decided that he must get into lower and warmer air. He throttled back the engines and put the plane into a shallow dive, and they gradually began to drop.

At 5,000 feet they were still in cloud and he wondered if it reached right down to sea-level. But the ice on the controls had begun to thaw, and at last, at 500 feet, they glided out of the cloud into clear air. Alcock opened up the engines and they responded normally again. They flew on, a few hundred feet above the sea, now searching the horizon for sight of land.

It came at last at 08.15 hours, when they sighted the mountains of Connemara, and they crossed the coast of Ireland close to the little town of Clifden at 08.25. They circled the town, and Brown fired two Very lights to attract attention.

They had originally planned to fly on to Brooklands, if possible, and they still had enough petrol to do so. But, probably feeling the strain of the flight by now, Alcock decided to land near Clifden. Close to the town was a wireless station, and near it what appeared to the flyers to be an expanse of green grass. Alcock headed for the station and circled it, firing red Very lights. He saw men pouring out of the station buildings, waving and gesticulating, but never guessed that they had seen his intention, and were trying to warn him off. The deceptive expanse of grass they had sighted was in reality the Derrygimla Bog, and as the Vimy landed on it the wheels skimmed over pools of slimy water and dug themselves into the soft ground. The plane stopped abruptly, the nose dug into the earth and the tail pointed skywards. The two occupants were saved from being flung out by their safety belts, and as rescuers came running from the wireless station, they slowly climbed out of their cockpit.

They had arrived safely in Ireland, and were the first aviators to cross the Atlantic non-stop. The journey of 1,880 miles had taken exactly fifteen hours fifty-seven minutes, giving an average speed of 118·5 miles per hour.

In more ways than one, Alcock and Brown were fortunate in landing close to a wireless station. The Marconi station at Clifden was a high-powered station for transatlantic communication. Within a few minutes of their landing the news was being broadcast all over the world. At St. John's the Vickers party heard the news from Mount Pearl station greatly to their relief. Since the Vimy had crossed the coast of Newfoundland there had been no message from it, and there had naturally been considerable concern for the flyers' safety. In Ireland, on the other hand, Brown and Alcock, as they sat at breakfast in the mess-room of the Marconi wireless station, were concerned lest the Handley Page V.1500 had made the crossing ahead of them. A wireless message to Mount Pearl elicited the reply that the V.1500 was still at Harbour Grace. In the event, it never made the attempt, but returned by sea, as also did Freddy Raynham and his aircraft.

Alcock and Brown had indubitably won the *Daily Mail* prize for the first direct crossing of the Atlantic.

They set off for London the following day, still in the clothes in which they had crossed the Atlantic; Arthur Whitten Brown in his uniform of a Flight-Lieutenant, Royal Air Force, and John Alcock, who never cared very much what he wore, in a blue suit and a cloth cap. All the way across Ireland they were received triumphantly; at every stop huge crowds had gathered to see them. In England it was the same, as the 'Irish Mail' pursued its way from Holyhead to Euston. In London the welcome given to Hawker and Mackenzie-Grieve was repeated and crowds cheered them all the way from the railway station to the headquarters of the Royal Aero Club.

The presentation of the *Daily Mail* prize took place on the following Friday, June 20th, at a luncheon at the Savoy Hotel. The Editor of the *Daily Mail* presided in place of Lord Northcliffe, who was in hospital, and after the customary speeches a cheque for £10,000 was presented to Alcock by Mr. Winston Churchill, at that time Home Secretary. He then announced that His Majesty King George V had authorised him to state that the order of Knight Commander of the Order of the British Empire would be conferred upon John Alcock and Arthur Whitten Brown.

For several weeks the two flyers were lionised wherever they went. When they went to Windsor to be knighted by King George, the boys of Eton College took the horses from their carriage and pulled it themselves. They were in demand at charity functions of every kind; wherever they went they were besieged by autograph hunters and hero-worshippers. Then in due course other attractions took their place, and they were able to slip back into a more normal existence.

John Alcock (Sir John, as he now was) resumed his work with Vickers as a test pilot. His career, sad to relate, was cut short. Like so many of his fellow-airmen of the pre-war period—Hawker, Hamel, Cody—he died while flying. Six months after his transatlantic flight, in December 1919, he made his last flight. He was to deliver, to an aeronautical exhibition being held in Paris, the latest aircraft from Vickers—the *Viking*. On the way, in bad visibility, he crashed near Rouen, and was killed. So ended the brief career of one of the foremost pilots of his time. He lived and died in an era which he himself epitomised, the era of the pioneer 'bird-men', of daring and adventure; an era which was rapidly giving way to the more hum-drum world of commercial flying.

Sir Arthur Whitten Brown gave up flying and returned to engineering. His dream of navigating the first aircraft across the Atlantic had been fulfilled, and that was sufficient for him. His way and that of Alcock's parted, and they never saw each other again.

Of the third character in the drama, the Vickers *Vimy*, the same could be said. Its brief career was ended, for it never flew again. A party of Vickers mechanics arrived at Clifden, hauled it out of the bog and dismantled it. It was returned to the works at Brooklands by train, and after repair was presented to the Science Museum at South Kensington. There it hangs today, a memorial to the daring, courage and endurance of its crew.

Another, and more recent, memorial can be seen at London Airport. In front of No. 3 building, within view of passengers boarding or alighting from their transatlantic planes, is a statue of the two airmen in flying kit. On the plinth beneath them is the following inscription:

SIR JOHN ALCOCK
AND
SIR ARTHUR WHITTEN BROWN
WHO MADE
THE FIRST DIRECT FLIGHT ACROSS THE ATLANTIC
VICKERS VIMY AIRCRAFT : ROLLS ROYCE ENGINES
ST. JOHN'S, NEWFOUNDLAND : CLIFDEN, IRELAND
14TH TO 15TH JUNE 1919

St. John's, like most cities, has spread its boundaries in the years since the Saturday afternoon when Alcock and Brown started on their epic flight. Lester's Field is a field no more, but is covered by rows of neat wooden suburban houses. At Clifden the Derrygimla Bog is still a bog, and in both places the story of the flight has passed into history as something which grandparents relate to their grandchildren.

CHAPTER 10

The Atlantic is Conquered

ALTHOUGH THE ATLANTIC had been successfully crossed by air, it was many years before a regular air service was established. There is a world of difference between a crossing by adventurers like Alcock and Brown or Hawker and Grieve, who chose the easier way—west to east; the most favourable time—mid June, and still risked their lives; and on the other hand a regular air service in fair weather and foul, carrying passengers in comfort and safety.

It was not until 1927 that the Atlantic was successfully flown from east to west. It was done by an Irishman, Colonel J. C. Fitzmaurice, and two Germans, Captain H. Kohl and Baron Von Hunefeld, flying in a Junkers monoplane. They set off from Ireland, carrying with them a letter from the President of the Irish Free State to the President of the United States of America. All went well until they were off the Newfoundland Grand Banks, when they ran into fog. They climbed to get above it, and ice formed on their wings, while high winds started to blow them off course. The old bogy of Atlantic weather was at work.

After flying blind for some time they came out into a clear star-filled sky. On the horizon the Northern Lights flashed. They flew on and at daylight saw below them a lighthouse. They landed beside it and found themselves in the snow of Greenly Island in the Straits of Belle Isle, just off the northernmost tip of Newfoundland. They had been in the air for fourteen hours and were the first to fly direct from Europe to America.

By 1932 the idea of a transatlantic air service was being seriously considered. At the Imperial Conference at Ottawa that year, representatives of Canada, Great Britain, and Newfoundland met to consider the matter, and a committee was set up to investigate the possibilities of an air-mail service. In 1933 the Prime Minister of Newfoundland was able to announce that an agreement had been concluded by which Imperial Airways would have the sole right to use air bases in Newfoundland for transatlantic flying for the next fifteen years.

In 1934 the point had been reached at which Imperial Airways decided to order two aircraft for the North Atlantic service. Specially constructed and equipped for the route, they were modified versions of the now famous Short *Empire* S.23 class. These were flying-boats fitted with four Bristol Pegasus X engines, giving a total horsepower of 3,640. They could cruise at 140 miles an hour, and carried twenty-four passengers. The two built for the transatlantic service were named *Caledonia* and *Cambria*.

The two principal difficulties which had to be overcome, and which, as we have seen, caused most of the trouble for the pioneer flyers, were the Atlantic weather and the problem of wireless communication. Added to these was the question of how a commercial aircraft could carry enough fuel to make the crossing in safety and still take an economic pay-load. One by one these problems were tackled and solved.

Over the years a detailed survey of weather conditions above the Atlantic was carried out by meteorologists stationed at points in Newfoundland, Labrador, and Iceland. Gradually a service was built up which could give pilots of aircraft accurate information about the weather they might expect, so that bad conditions could be avoided where possible. In this way the first problem was gradually mastered. The problem of wireless communication was solved as equipment improved with time, and as more stations were set up on both sides of the Atlantic. The object was to ensure that an aircraft could not only keep in touch with the ground while in flight, but could also be told of its position, obtained by 'fixes' from ground stations. The uncertainties which had magnified the risks taken by the early flyers were slowly and scientifically eliminated. There still remained the problem of the pay-load.

This problem resolves itself into the matter of getting the aircraft and its load of fuel off the ground. Once in the air it can support a load much greater than that which it can lift. Two different methods were tried in order to get over this difficulty. The first was distinctly novel, and remains unique in the history of flight. It involved the use of the Short-Mayo composite aircraft. This was a 'pick-a-back' system consisting of a specially adapted S.23 *Empire* flying-boat (named the *Maia*) which had mounted on its back a twin-float seaplane (the *Mercury*). The two aircraft took off fastened together, and the *Maia* carried the heavily loaded *Mercury* to the required height, where a release mechanism was operated and the two aircraft separated, the seaplane to fly on its way, and the flying boat to return to its base. In this way the maximum weight of cargo could be carried.

The system was used for the first commercial flight across the Atlantic. In July 1938 the *Mercury* flew from Shannon, in Ireland, direct to Montreal, a distance of 3,000 miles. On this experimental flight the cargo consisted of half a ton of newspapers, photographs, and newsreels of the visit of King George VI and Queen Elizabeth to Paris. Although successful, the experiment was not pursued, as it was not an economical way of operating and in addition it was felt that the experience would be too alarming to commend itself to passengers.

The other method, which has since become common practice but was then in its infancy, was the system of flight refuelling. By this method an aircraft can take off with a light load of fuel and when it has gained the required height in the air it is filled up from a tanker aircraft flying above it, the connection being made by means of a flexible hose which is trailed behind the tanker. In the end it was this system which was adopted.

While all this experimental work was being carried out, preparations were also being made in Newfoundland for a transatlantic service. At Botwood, in the north of the island, and on the mouth of the Exploits River, a seaplane base was set up. Botwood is a busy port in summer, and through it goes the newsprint from the mills at Grand Falls. In 1937 it was the western terminus of the sea crossing.

Some thirty miles away, on the Great Gander Lake, an airfield was built to accommodate the landplanes which would be required to act as tankers for those flying-boats making the west to east crossing. Today Gander airport is international in scope, a crossroads of the world connected to most parts of the northern hemisphere by air. In 1937 it was still being hacked out of the pine forests which surround it.

All this preliminary work took time, and in the meanwhile Germany had introduced a form of Atlantic airmail. This was done by fitting two large liners, the *Bremen* and *Europa*, with aircraft catapults. A seaplane was carried, and half way across the Atlantic the seaplane would be flown off with the mails, which would thus arrive well in advance of the liner, saving considerable time. The seaplane would then be picked up for the return trip.

The British Government were sufficiently worried by this competition to meet and discuss with the Canadian authorities the possibility of an airmail service from Canada to Newfoundland and from Ireland to London, with a fast steamship service between Newfoundland and Ireland. (Shades of Sandford Fleming!) No such arrangement was concluded, however; instead, work was concentrated on a transatlantic air service.

By July 1937 everything was at last ready for an experimental service to begin. On the 5th of that month the flying-boat *Caledonia*, G-ADHM, piloted by Captain Wilcockson, left Foynes in Ireland for Botwood, Newfoundland. The flight was uneventful, as the following extracts from the W/T log show.*

18.57   G.M.T. Caledonia, Wilcockson, departed Foynes for Botwood. Control officer Foynes.

23.10   G-ADHM calling. We have been in touch with *New York City* in Lat. 62.36 N, Long. 17.35 W. He gave me bearing 224 degrees and think this bearing was relative to his ship's head and not true bearing, so am going to change wave to 600 metres to check again.

00.00   G-ADHM calling. Position midnight 51.40 N, 23.22 W. Total darkness, 10/10 cloud.

00.33   NF.15 Botwood calling G-ADHM. Your bearing is 67 degrees doubtful at 00.33 G.M.T.

04.29   G-ADHM calling. Marked VCE (Cape Race) on 600 metres.

06.30   G-ADHM calling. Position 06.30, 50.25 N, 44.40 W, over cloud.

09.30   NF.15 Botwood calling. Latest of G-ADHM passed coast of Newfoundland 09.20.

10.13   NF.15 Botwood calling. G-ADHM Wilcockson landed Botwood 10.00 G.M.T, moored 10.13.

It will be noticed that the *Caledonia* was in touch with her New-

* Imperial Airways Gazette IX No. 8, August 5th–6th, 1937.

foundland base at Botwood for the greater part of the flight. In mid-Atlantic she passed in the darkness the Pan-American flying boat *Clipper III*, which was making the first commercial flight from west to east. The whole business of Atlantic crossing had become routine.

Preparations now went ahead for a regular weekly air service to Montreal via Botwood. Four more flying-boats were ordered. These were launched in 1939 and were named *Cabot, Caribou, Connemara* and *Clyde*, the first two names having obvious associations with Newfoundland. In addition three Handley Page *Harrow* landplanes were purchased and converted into tankers. Two were shipped out to Gander by sea, a method of travel reminiscent of their forebear, the V.1500 of 1919, which travelled out to Newfoundland and back by surface transport.

At last, on July 5th, 1939, the North Atlantic air service for passengers and mails was opened when the *Caribou*, piloted by Captain Rogers, flew from Foynes to Botwood. It was just over 20 years since Alcock and Brown had made their epic flight. Now at last passengers could travel in comfort and safety over the ocean which the early flyers had traversed at their peril.

But the new service was short-lived. With the outbreak of war in August of the same year, it was suspended, and the flying-boats went into war service with the R.A.F. Coastal Command. Their reign had been short, and they never returned. During the war it was found to be possible to fly landplanes regularly across the ocean. Bombers built in the U.S.A. and Canada were flown over to Britain, and air crews were ferried back. The meteorological and wireless systems, painstakingly built up in the pre-war years, were of course an enormous advantage to the war effort. They were improved and enlarged, and the airport at Gander also, so that it became a staging post between Europe and America for the constant stream of military traffic. On the other side of the ocean a similar airport was built at Prestwick, in Scotland, large enough to take the biggest aircraft flying.

When the war ended all the requirements for operating an air service across the Atlantic existed, and a tremendous store of experience had been built up. But it was a landplane service now, and the flying-boats were no longer required. And that is how it has developed to this day, so that now giant jet airliners fly above Atlantic storms in the sunshine, and land at Gander six hours after leaving Prestwick.

Perhaps someone will read these words while flying on just such a flight, while sipping an aperetif and waiting for the attractive air hostess to bring dinner. If so, spare a thought for the heroes that made it possible: John Alcock wrestling to control his lumbering *Vimy* in the storms far below; Arthur Whitten Brown, the cripple, crawling over the wing 9,000 feet above the Atlantic to free the engines of ice; Hawker and Mackenzie-Grieve searching desperately for a ship as their overheated engine begins to stutter. Or, to go further back still, think of the men who risked their lives in the *Agamemnon* through the fury of Atlantic gales to lay the slender thread that united the two continents for the first time; and the persistence of the men of the *Great Eastern* as they grappled for the lost cable again and again; and failed and then went back to start all over again. Behind the smooth efficiency of modern communications of land, sea or air lies a tremendous story of human endeavour.

BIBLIOGRAPHY

Among others, I have consulted the following publications during the writing of this book:

NARRATIVE OF A JOURNEY ACROSS THE ISLAND OF NEWFOUNDLAND, by W. E. McCormack, 1822
HISTORY OF NEWFOUNDLAND, by Daniel Prowse, 1893
THE ATLANTIC TELEGRAPH, by W. E. Russell, 1865
THE ATLANTIC CABLE, by Charles Bright, 1903
NEWFOUNDLAND IN 1911, by P. J. McGrath
THE ATLANTIC CABLE, by Bern Dibner, 1953
SANDFORD FLEMING, EMPIRE BUILDER, by L. Burpee, 1915
MARCONI, THE MAN AND HIS WIRELESS, by Orin E. Dunlap, 1936
THE FLIGHT OF ALCOCK AND BROWN, by Graham Wallace, 1956
BRITAIN'S IMPERIAL AIR ROUTES; 1918-1939, by Robin Higham, 1959
ONE HUNDRED YEARS OF SUBMARINE CABLES, the Science Museum, 1950
CANADIAN NATIONAL RAILWAYS: A SYNOPTIC HISTORY, by J. Kearney, 1962
REPORT ON THE INTERCOLONIAL RAILWAY (White Paper), by Sandford Fleming, 1864
DECISIONS OF THE SUPREME COURT OF NEWFOUNDLAND, edited by J. B. Morris, 1897
BENJAMIN BOWRING AND HIS DESCENDANTS, by A. Wardle, 1940
PRIVY COUNCIL JUDICIAL COMMITTEE LAW REPORTS
The Times
The Daily Mail
The Illustrated London News
The Newfoundland Royal Gazette
The Daily News, St. John's
The Evening Telegram, St. John's

INDEX

Agamemnon, H.M.S., 33, 39
Albany, S.S., 70, 75
A. L. Blackman (locomotive), 101, 111
Alcock, Sir John, 169 et seq.
America Airship, 153 et seq.
Amherst, Colonel, 12
Anderson, Capt. (*Great Eastern*), 63, 76
Anglo-American Telegraph Co., 69, 149
Anglo-Newfoundland Development Co., 124
Atlantic Charter, signing, 116
Atlantic Telegraph Co., 30, 32
Avalon Peninsula, 11

Baldwin Locomotive Co., 117
Bay Bulls (cable terminus), 42, 51, 123
Berryman, Lieut. U.S.N., 28
Biscay, Bay of (cable tests), 38
Blackman, Albert, 101, 109
Bond, Sir Robert, 147
Botwood Airport, 185 et seq.
Bowaters Ltd., 127
Bowring, Benjamin, 134, 147
Boyle, Sir Cavendish, 144, 147
Brassey, Thomas, 58, 61
Brett, John, 23, 30
Bright, Sir Charles, 26
British North America Act 1867, 97
Brown, Sir Arthur Whitten, 171
Bruce S.S., 119
Brunel, Isambard Kingdom, 29, 59
Buchanan, President James, 51

C-5 Airship, 162
Cabot Tower, 135, 144 et seq.
Caledonia Flight, 186
Canadian Pacific Ralway, 98, 100
Canning, Samuel, 35
Cape Breton, 21

Cape Cod Wireless Station, 142
Cape Race, 28
Cape Ray, 21, 27
Caribou (train), 121 et seq.
Carlisle, Earl of, 36
Caroline S.S., 63
Chain Rock, 12, 110, 133
Clarendon, Lord, 30
Clifden, Ireland, 179
Coherer, 138
Coil, Lt. Cmdr. U.S.N., 162
Cooper, Peter, 24, 27
Cormack, W. E., 17 et seq., 92
Cornerbrook, 127
Cows on railway lines, 116
Crookes, Sir William, 136
Curtiss Flying Boats, 161, 163
Cyclops, H.M.S., 29

Daily Mail Prize, 157 et seq., 180
Davenport & Pierson, Messrs., 110
De Sauty, Mr., 63, 66

Edward, Prince of Wales (Edward VII), 63, 140
1858 Cable, 32 (description), 41 (splicing), 50 (completion), 52 (first message), 54 (failure)
1865 Atlantic Cable, 58 (description), 67 (loss of), 76 (completion)
1866 Atlantic cable, 70 et seq.
Empire S-23 flying boats, 184
Ericson, Leif, 12
Evans, Francis, 115
Everett, Edward, 35

Field, Cyrus, 22 et seq., 56, 63, 79
First transatlantic flight, 176 et seq.
Fitzmaurice, Col. J. C., 183
Fleming, Professor Sir Ambrose, 139, 142
Fleming, Sir Sandford, 84 et seq., 98

INDEX

Flying Huntress, S.S., 139
Fort William station, 110, 119
Foxtrap, battle of, 107
'French Shore', 100

Gander Airport, 124, 185
George, Prince (George V), 113
Ghost train, 125
Gilbert, Sir Humphrey, 12
Gisborne, Frederic Newton, 21 et seq., 24, 77, 101
Glass, Elliott & Co., 26, 32
Gooch, Sir Daniel, 61, 69
Gorgon H.M.S., 49
Great American & European Short Line Railway Co., 102, 111, 114
Great Eastern, S.S., 29, 59 et seq., 88
Gutta Percha Co., 26, 32

Hall's Bay, 107, 118 (railway)
Halpin, Capt. Robert (*Great Eastern*), 78
Handley Page V.1500 aircraft, 169
Harbour Grace, 107, 160, 169
Hawker and Grieve, 160, 164 et seq.
Hawthorn and Co., 112
Heart's Content, 71, 77, 107
Hertz, Heinreich, 136
Hon. Robert Bond (locomotive), 119
Howlett, Conductor Stephen, 119
Hudson, Capt. U.S.N., 36, 50
'Human wind gauge', 128

Intercolonial railway, 89 et seq.

Johnson, President Andrew, 72

Kelvin, Lord (Professor W. Thompson), 32
Kemp, Mr. G. S., 143
Kerry, Knight of, 36, 48
Keyham Basin, 37
Kinniple & Morris, Messrs., 107

Lester's Field, 174
Locomotive preserved at Bowater Park, 127

Lodge, Sir Oliver, 136
London & Birmingham Railway, 18

Macdonald, Sir John, 87, 88, 97
Magnetic Telegraph Co., 29, 31
Maia-Mercury aircraft, 184
Mackay, A. M., 27, 150
Marconi, Guglielmo, 136 et seq.
Maury, Lieut. Matthew U.S.N., 23
Maxwell, Professor Clerk, 135
Medway S.S., 70, 75
Mirror galvanometer, 52, 64
Morse, Professor Samuel, 22
Mullock, Bishop, 19 et seq., 106

Narrows, The, 11, 133
Needles wireless station, 140
New York, Newfoundland and London Electric Telegraph Co., 24
Newall and Co., 32
Newcastle, Duke of, 87, 89
Newfoundland & North Western Railway, 118, 119
Newfoundland Electric Telegraph Co., 21, 24
Newfoundland Museum, 72, 77, 164
Newfoundland Railway Co., 109
Niagara, U.S.S., 34, 123
Niger H.M.S., 71
Northern Railroad, 85

Otter, Capt., R.N., 49

Paget, Mr. P. W., 143
Placentia, 116
Poldhu Wireless Station, 142
Porcupine, H.M.S., 49
Port-aux-Basques, 119, 128
Porte, Lieut., 158
Prince Edward Island Railway, 110
Privy Council, 56, 115
Prowse, Judge Daniel, 27, 108

Quidi Vidi Lake, 50, 162, 173

INDEX

Racoon, H.M.S., 70
Railway Commission (Newfoundland), 107, 109
'Raymor' aircraft, 164 et seq.
Raynham and Morgan, 160, 165
Red River Settlement, 86
Reid, Sir Robert, 117 et seq., 120
Roberts, Marshall, 24
Royal Newfoundland Regt., 159
Russell, William, 63

St. Georges Bay, 98
St. John's (City), 11, 133
St. John's (locomotive), 112
Sarah L. Bryant, S.S., 26
Siemens, Dr. Werner, 33
Signal Hill, 133 et seq., 144
Siphon Recorder, 73
Sir Herbert Murray (locomotive), 119
Sopwith *Atlantic* aircraft, 163
Sphinx, H.M.S., 63, 65

Taylor, Moses, 24
Telegraph Construction & Maintenance Co., 58, 61
Telegraphic Plateau, 29

Terrible, H.M.S., 63, 66, 70, 75
Thorburn, Sir Robert, 116
'Tin-can' mail, 28
Topsails, The, 125 et seq.
Total Abstinence Society excursion, 112
Towers, Commander J. H., U.S.N., 163
Trans-Canada Highway, 128
Trepassey, 161
Trinity Bay, 49

Valentia, cable-laying at, 36, 47
Vickers *Vimy* bomber, 153, 171
Victoria, H.M. Queen, 51, 72
Victoria, S.S., 19, 26

Wellman, Walter, 153 et seq
Wheatstone, Charles, 18
White, Chandler, 24
Whitehouse, Dr. William, 32, 53
Whiteway, Sir William, 105, 117
William Cory, S.S. ('Dirty Billy'), 70
Wireless Telegraph & Signal Co., 139
'Wire Squadron', The, 36, 38
Wood, Nicolas, 38 et seq.